Capturing
VENICE

Planning and executing great travel photography

MAIN GUIDE

James Dugan

www.walkaboutphotoguides.com

Copyright and disclaimer

Map legends

Throughout the guide, you will see these symbols in maps and some other parts as well. We've compiled it here for your easy reference!

Attraction	Photo opportunity
Bridge	Synagogue
Cemetery	Ticket Office
Church	Tower
Monument	Theatre
Museum	Town Square

Reader bonuses

As a thank you to readers of this guide, we have some bonuses to help you plan and execute a great travel photography trip to Venice:

Free eBook "Managing your camera equipment and images"

This eBook is packed with practical tips on ensuring that you get the best performance out of your cameras, and how to manage your images when you are on the ground.

Access to the photos in the guide

You can now get access to large-size versions of all of the images found in the guide.

How-to guide for Google Maps list

Step-by-step (with screenshots) guide to creating a custom Google Maps list. We've also included access to the Google Maps list that we've used for Venice as well!

For your free bonuses, head over to

walkaboutphotoguides.com/venice/guidebonus/

About our guides

Our guides help you maximise your time on the ground to get a great set of photos. This guide walks you through the planning and logistics that go into a productive and enjoyable trip to take photos in Venice.

Taking a trip with the express intention of taking photos can be different to a regular trip in a few important ways. The biggest difference is chasing the best light for your subjects – good light is often the secret sauce to capturing a compelling image. Here are some of the key considerations for a productive trip:

Timing

Structure your visits to specific locations to coincide with the best light conditions. This means becoming flexible with your schedule, particularly if you have to work with variable weather conditions.

Pacing

"Working" a subject / location for the best images takes time. This is often a lot more than the average non-photographer travel companion is likely to be able to put up with!

Walking

There is likely to be a fair bit of walking involved, which may take some getting used to. This is a particularly important consideration if you don't normally exercise.

Early starts

Getting up in time to photograph sunrise has two huge benefits – you capture some of the best light of the day on your surroundings, and you are often likely to have the place to yourself whilst everybody else is still in bed. Depending on the time of year, you will need to get up earlier than usual to be in position for a sunrise.

Sunset

This can often overlap with dinner times, so eating earlier or later than normal is probably going to occur.

May you have fantastic light, full camera batteries, and fill up your memory cards!

Frequently asked questions

The Frequently Asked Questions (FAQ) below allow you to dive straight into the guide.

Q: Where is the information about hotels, bars, restaurants, and shopping found in other travel guides?

A: Our guides are focused on providing you with the information you need to hit the ground and take good photos. We emphasise this with detailed maps and diagrams, photos, camera settings, and lots of logistical information. This is where we have invested our time through research and boots on the ground. Being perfectly honest - hotels, bars, restaurants, and shopping options change fairly often, and it is a huge effort keeping this information current. We trust that our readers are comfortable with making their accommodation bookings online through aggregators, as well as reading up-to-date reviews for bars and restaurants. And we assume that if you're already lugging all of your photography gear, there's not much room left for the shopping!

Q: How does this guide differ from a photography tour?

A: Photography tours are a fantastic way to have a local photographer show you about the city and share with you their secret shooting spots. They are also able to provide you with on-the-spot tips and advice to improve the quality of your photos taken. Tour guides can help with translation as required. Lastly, having others around, particularly a local, can allay fears of attracting unwanted attention.

However, you do need to pay for the photographer's valuable time. You'll also need to book them in advance and agree a time that works for both of you (assuming you don't have to join a small group where the time will be dictated already). Hopefully the weather conditions are favourable during your booking!

Our guides provide much of this knowledge and insight whilst allowing you to be flexible with your time and allow for potentially changing weather conditions.

If possible, consider both a photo tour and our guide as they are natural complements.

Q: Any tips on where I should stay during my visit?

A: Read of our section on accommodation (page 186), including how to optimise for best photo opportunities.

Q: How can I make sure that I get the best shots?

A: So many factors affect the success of your trip, however you can stack the deck in your favour:

When to go (page 181) - Know the best time(s) of the year for good light and minimal rain.

Photo tips and tricks - For each of the main sites described in this guide, there is a section on photo tips and tricks so you can skip right to there to get started.

Q: Are there walking tours of Venice?

A: There are indeed, including walks covering specific parts of the city, as well as night time "ghost" tours. Although not particularly easy to photograph, the night tours are best for evoking images of what life was like during the plagues or times when alleyways were teeming with robbers and ne'er do wells.

Q: Do I need a car to see Venice?

A: No! With the exception of the Lido, all of Venice is gloriously car-free. Your main modes of transport are your feet (page 191) or the *vaporetto* water ferries (page 192).

200mm, f/8, ISO 100, 1/500 sec
FF camera
1.00
The viewing platform of the Campanile, the best elevated view point in Venice.

Contents

Welcome
to Venice

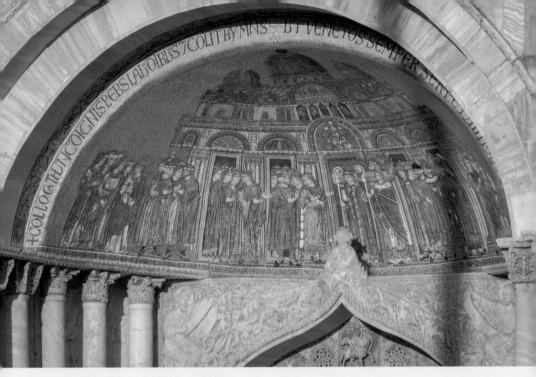

1.01   200mm, f/8, ISO 160, 1/320 sec FF camera   Mosaic depicting the spiriting away of the body of St Mark outside of the Basilica.

Introduction

One of the truly amazing cities of the world, Venice has captured imaginations (and hearts) for centuries. This lagoon city has something for every type of photographer, from architecture to street photography. And, if you do some extra planning, it makes for an excellent location for fashion and portraiture photography as well.

In addition to seeking out great photo opportunities, don't miss the chance to take in the rest of what the city has to offer, including:

Museums and galleries (page 115) - Venice has a cornucopia of museums and galleries that are waiting for you to explore. For art buffs, many originals of the Italian masters are still exhibited in the place that their creator intended. This means that you'll probably find yourself ducking into many of the city's churches along the way.

Local cuisine (page 171) - Venetian cuisine emphasises its connection with the sea, with many dishes only prepared when the fish or vegetables are in season.

Daily life (page 174) - It can sometimes be easy to forget that Venice is actually home to around 50,000 fulltime residents. If you venture away from the crowds, you can gain an appreciation of the joys (and struggles) of living on the water.

It's very easy to be trapped behind the viewfinder and not enjoy the centuries of history and the rise and fall of the Venetian Republic and its legacies. To truly enjoy the wonders of Venice, put your camera away from time to time and allow yourself to just soak it in!

Photo themes

Venice has more sites than you can reasonably poke a camera lens at during a single visit. In order to maximise your opportunities to get great photos in a short space of time, here's the best places to focus on (pun intended!) to go.

105mm, f/5.6, ISO 200, 1/160 sec
FF camera

1.02 The eponymous "plague doctor" costume is often on display outside tourist-oriented shops.

▌ Sunrises

Apart from the lovely colours that slowly creep across the city from the East, sunrise is your chance to have Venice (largely) to yourself. Check out our accommodation tips (page 186) to make getting up early a little bit easier. Standout sunrise locations include:

· **Piazza San Marco** (page 16) - The one time of the day that the piazza is free from throngs of tourists, touts, and restaurants spilling into the piazza. The sunrise lights up Torre dell'Orologio (page 34) as shadows slowly fade away across the piazza.

· **Riva degli Schiavoni** (page 59) - A great vantage point for watching the sun rise up behind Basilica di San Giorgio Maggiore (page 70).

· **Ponte dell'Accademia** (page 61) - The newly restored bridge makes for an excellent vantage point to shoot the first rays coming up behind Basilica di Santa Maria della Salute (page 75).

· **Isola di San Giorgio Maggiore** (page 70) - For the most front-facing view of the sun coming up on Palazzo Ducale (page 38), get an early morning *vaporetto* here.

· **Punta della Dogana** (page 101) - A little more of an oblique angle of Palazzo Ducale than Isola di San Giorgio Maggiore (above), the point at the end of the island affords panoramic views around the lagoon.

· **Trinita water taxi pier** (page 73) - This secret location is great for getting canal-level views of Basilica di San Giorgio Maggiore (page 70) and Punta della Dogana (page 101) as the sun comes up.

Sunsets

Sunsets over Venice can be dramatic, and it's also a great time to watch the city transition from the mania of the day into the much calmer evenings / nights. Stand-out sunset locations include:

· **Campanile di San Marco** (page 28) - Hands-down the best place to capture sunset over Venice, with 360 degrees panoramas and places to balance your camera for long-exposures.

· **Ponte di Rialto** (page 57) - Facing West (the busy side), you can watch the gondolas ferrying their last customers of the day, and the Grand Canal calms to a quieter pace in the evening. You will need to exercise a bit of patience and vigilance with finding a spot for photos, and you'll need to keep an eye on your belongings because of the crowds.

· **Piazza San Marco** (page 16) - Time your arrival to be at least an hour before sunset so that you can capture the effect of the sun on the gold tiles that adorn the Basilica. Don't wait too long as the sun quickly disappears behind the shadows cast by Museo Correr and the rear of the piazza.

· **Riva degli Schiavoni** (page 59) - Just around the corner from Piazza San Marco, here you can watch the sun set over Isola di San Giorgio Maggiore. Bring your tripod to capture long exposure shots of gondolas bobbing up and down in the water in the foreground with the Basilica as the backdrop.

· **Punta della Dogana** (page 101) - Similar to sunrise, the versatility of this location at the very tip of Dorsoduro isn't to be underestimated as a sunset spot. Don't forget the tripod as the evening moves into the blue hour (just after sunset).

Architecture

Venice has long been famous for its architectural marvels, riffing on Byzantine, Gothic, Renaissance, and Baroque styles, all with a distinct Venetian flare. Stand-out architecture includes:

· **Basilica di San Marco** (page 22) - The showpiece of Venice for centuries, the Basilica even drew the ire of the Catholic church and so was officially the "private" church of the Doge. Explore the interior as well (page 22).

· **Palazzo Ducale** (page 38) - With its distinct colouring and style, the house of the Doges and epicentre of government is a must-see for photos. The interiors are equally impressive, considering the scale of some of the rooms and halls.

· **Ca d'Oro** (page 116) - Considered the epitome of Venetian Gothic architecture, it has influenced copies and imitators all over the world.

· **Scala Contarini del Bovolo** (page 110) - The famous multi-arch staircase, whose name translates as "of the snail", is visible from the courtyard of Palazzo Contarini del Bovolo.

· **Ponte di Rialto** (page 57) - Venice's most famous bridges, considered an engineering marvel at its time of construction. Even today, the wide-span bridge strikes a superb balance between connecting San Marco and San Polo as well as allowing water traffic to flow unabated.

· **Chiesa di Santa Maria dei Miracoli** (page 85) - Looking like a cute music box from the outside, the barrel vault design (i.e. lack of pillars) inside makes this Renaissance church stand out amongst the Venetian crowd.

· **Biennale pavilions** (page 121) - For those in search of modern architectural designs, check out the buildings constructed for the Venice Biennale.

History

· **Palazzo Ducale** (page 38) - The numerous halls of the *palazzo* are filled with art, treasures, armoury, and maps of the world under the Venetian Empire. Don't forget to check out the lesser-seen photo opportunities that come with the two Secret Itineraries tours (page 44).

· **Arsenale di Venezia** (page 104) and **Museo Storico Navale** (page 115) - Appreciate the maritime prowess that Venice established, with what was once the world's largest shipyard and an impressive array of barges.

· **Torcello** (page 133) - Now relegated to the back pages of history, Torcello was the birthplace of what has now become Venice. Basilica di Santa Maria Assunta (page 133) provides an impressive glimpse back to earlier times.

· **Isola di San Michele** (page 136) - Since Napoleon's reign, this island pair (merged)

has played host to a who's who of former residents of Venice.

· **Ghetto Nuovo** (page 107) - The Jewish community of Venice had been maligned long before the horrific events of the Second World War. A visit to the Museo Ebraico di Venezia (page 194) and surrounding synagogues provides a comprehensive history of the area.

Street photography

It is easy to feel that you are walking around in an open-air museum in Venice, with street photo opportunities just around each canal. Have a read of the section on the daily life of Venetians (page 178) for several ideas. In addition, for people and crowds, head to the following public spaces:

· Piazza San Marco (page 120).
· Campo Santo Stefano (page 169).
· Campo Santa Maria Formosa (page 170).
· Campo San Giacomo dell'Orio (page 170).
· Campo Santa Margherita (page 170).

80mm, f/11, ISO 200, 1/250 sec
FF camera

1.03 Afternoon shadows over the clock face of Torre dell'Orologio.

1.04   16mm, f/11, ISO 100, 1/320 sec CF 1.5x camera   The piazza from the balcony of Basilica di San Marco, looking out to the lagoon.

Piazza San Marco area

The centre of Venice, Piazza San Marco (St Mark's Square) is both beautiful and frustrating in equal measure! It has the honour of being the only place designated as a piazza (square) throughout Venice; other public spaces are relegated to the more common *campi* (fields). The gold-covered Basilica di San Marco (St Mark's Basilica) captivates with its impressive facades, as does its adjoining *campanile* (bell tower).

Almost hidden amongst the crowd, the Torre dell'Orologio (clock tower) on the North East end showcases the maritime priorities of the city on the clock face. On the South Eastern corner, the Palazzo Ducale (Doge's Palace) was the epicentre of Venetian power for many centuries.

Daytime crowds, pigeons, and mouthwatering food, this is a remarkable part of the city to spend some time. Gawk at the architecture, indulge in some people watching, and get some great images!

Piazza San Marco

Piazza San Marco (also known as St Mark's Square) is the beating heart of Venice. A famous quote, often attributed to Napoleon, describes the Piazza as the "drawing room of Europe". A fitting tribute, as Piazza San Marco showcases the city's affluent and powerful past. Named after the stunning and unique Basilica at the East end of the square, it has been the centre of Venetian life - from executions, proclamations, fairs, tournaments, and even religious celebrations.

▌Architecture and layout

A public place has existed in the piazza in some form since the 9th century, expanding and changing shape over time. The columns of San Marco and San Theodoro along the water's edge mark the historical entrance to the city.

These columns served as waypoints for mariners and traders to anchor along the shore. They would typically then proceed through the *Torre dell'Orologio* (clock tower) along the *Merceria* path (still visible to today) to the Rialto, the financial and market centre of town.

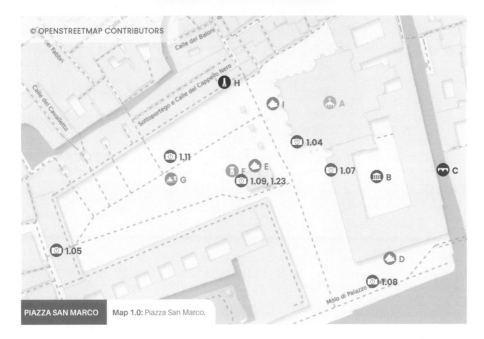

Map 1.0: Piazza San Marco.

The North side of the piazza is lined by the *Procuratie Vecchie* (Old Procuracies), the original homes of the Procurators of St Mark (officers of the Venetian Republic), built in the 16th century. To the North East, alongside the Basilica is the *Piazzetta dei Leoncini*, named for the two lion statues (the symbol of Venice). To the South side of the piazza, the *Procuratie Nuove* (New Procuracies) were constructed, stretching around the corner to the water to *Piazzetta San Marco*.

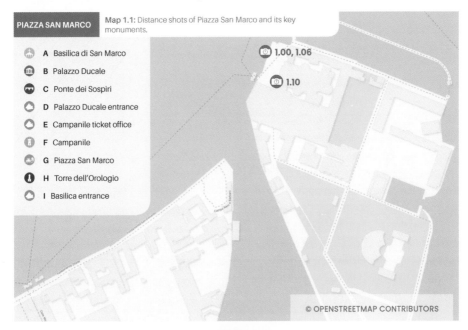

Map 1.1: Distance shots of Piazza San Marco and its key monuments.

- **A** Basilica di San Marco
- **B** Palazzo Ducale
- **C** Ponte dei Sospiri
- **D** Palazzo Ducale entrance
- **E** Campanile ticket office
- **F** Campanile
- **G** Piazza San Marco
- **H** Torre dell'Orologio
- **I** Basilica entrance

50mm, f/8, ISO 100, 1/400 sec
FF camera
1.07 The piazza from the balcony of Palazzo Ducale, accessible during the Secret Itineraries tour.

Logistics

Location information

 Piazza San Marco

 San Marco

 #piazzasanmarco,
#piazzasanmarcovenezia,
#piazzasanmarcos (!), #stmarkssquare

Beat the crowd

For fans of large, uncoordinated, confused crowds, look no further! Navigating through the piazza during the day can be a test of your coordination and patience. If you want the piazza (almost) to yourself, visit before 07:00 (regardless of the time of year) or around midnight. If you time your morning visit with sunrise, you can capture great images of the sun slowly lighting up the piazza from the East.

Pigeons

Pigeons are ever-present and the local police pursue those who try to feed them. Since 2008 it has been illegal to feed the pigeons, and attracts fines ranging from €70 to €700. Having said that, traditionally Venetians have been partial to the birds and used to feed their neighbourhood flocks. In addition, pigeon didn't historically feature on the Venetian menu either.

Flooding

The *acqua alta* is an ever-present threat to the city. The upside of any minor flooding into the square is that it can create a magical reflective surface. This might require a few photos to capture one with the water sufficiently still – there are always people mad enough to wade through water!

Prices

Restaurants facing onto the square have a reputation for charging a hefty premium for the privilege of the view of the square and the people-watching opportunities. If you are in any way budget conscious (i.e. you don't

24mm, f/11, ISO 100, 1/5 sec
FF camera
1.08 Long-exposure shot of evening in the *piazza*.

24mm, f/11, ISO 400, 1/5 sec
FF camera
1.09 Sunset over the piazza from the *campanile*.

consider $20 notes to be change), take a look at the menu before committing to food or even drinks. This can avoid the wallet shock that comes when the bill arrives, even for a bottle of water.

Photo tips and tricks

People-free piazza

Early rise - As noted above, you can get fairly people-free photos of the square in the early morning, particularly before 07:00. The earlier, the better.

Telephoto lens - This option works well during the day, particularly if you want sunlight on buildings. Use a telephoto lens and stand a distance from your subject. Patiently wait to get a shot when nobody is walking past, which becomes much easier when the angle of view that you're focusing on remains small. In addition, when using a telephoto lens from a distance, the "falling backwards" look of buildings in photos taken from a ground height perspective is reduced.

Angle above the crowd - If your interest is primarily in the architecture, consider angling your camera slightly upwards and take the photos before opening times for the sites (typically 09:30-10:00). There are less people milling about anyway, so you may even capture shots from the ground level without humans in shot.

Vantage points

There are many places that you can to get photos of the whole piazza including:

Basilica di San Marco - Emerging out on the balconies of the Basilica puts you front and centre of the crowds of the piazza.

Torre dell'Orologio - Accessing the roof top affords views across the piazza towards the lagoon. It is also possible to spy the piazza

200mm, f/11, ISO 100, 1/250 sec
CF 1.5x camera

1.10 Using a telephoto lens to photograph the piazza from the lagoon.

through the porthole windows on the lower levels.

Campanile di San Marco - The top of the bell tower has the best bird's eye view of the piazza (as well as the rest of Venice).

Palazzo Ducale - Similar to the views from the Basilica, check out the piazza views from the *loggia* (covered balconies). The best views are included as part of the Secret Itineraries tours (page 44).

Basilica di San Giorgio Maggiore - Stand outside of the basilica, just as you exit the *vaporetto* service, and face Piazza San Marco. This view looks straight through the two columns to the clock tower. Best views are in the morning (with the Eastern sun) using a decent telephoto lens to bridge the distance.

Night photos

There are many night time photo opportunities of the buzz of the place, as well as the buildings all lit up. Using a tripod in the square is straightforward, and you don't get hassled by security personnel.

Note: there is a current trend of street sellers trying to sell these glow-in-the-dark helicopter / propeller devices which zoom quickly high into the air and then take around 3-4 seconds to slowly come down to the ground. This means that long exposure shots can end up with blue light streaks of these devices. If this is of particular concern, either you can Photoshop the light trails out later, or simply take the photos late into the night (after 23:00) when the sellers have packed up for the night.

90mm, f/8, ISO 800, 1/100 sec
FF camera
1.11   Piazza San Marco in the afternoons is great for photos of crowds.

 28mm, f/11, ISO 1000, 1/320 sec
FF camera
The domes of the Basilica at sunset, seen from the nearby *campanile*.

1.12

Basilica di San Marco

Dominating Piazza San Marco, Basilica di San Marco is one of the most admired symbols of the artistic and architectural beauty of Italy. It has it all: elegance, wonderful Italo-Byzantine style and by sumptuous decorations of mosaics, marbles, columns and sculptures.

▌ Architecture and layout

What started out as the Doge of Venice's private chapel (next door to the palace) easily eclipsed the official cathedral of the city, Basilica di San Pietro in Castello. Twice rebuilt, the Greek cross layout design has remained (largely) intact from 1094 CE.

Façade

The breathtaking five niches and mosaics are a sight to behold and provide the viewer a taste of what is to come inside.

The mosaics inside the niches depict the story of St Mark, the patron saint of Venice, whose body was spirited away from Egypt back to Venice. His body was stored in pig fat to avoid the Muslim Egyptians inspecting the body.

Mosaics and depictions

The interior is deliberately imposing, with its three naves and three domes inspired by the Church of the Holy Apostles in Constantinople. The gilded mosaics earned the basilica the nickname *Chiesa d'Oro* (Church of Gold). The shimmering effect of the mosaics comes from the tesserae using a gold "sandwich" technique (gold leaf between two layers of glass). Some of the key mosaics and features to keep an eye out for (further information is available inside the basilica):

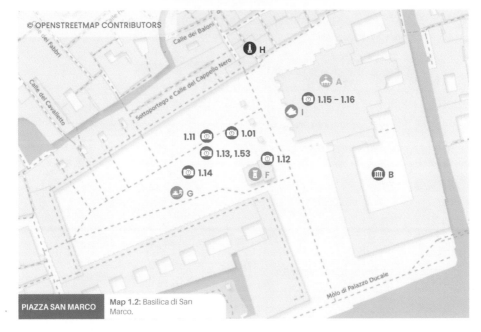

© OPENSTREETMAP CONTRIBUTORS

PIAZZA SAN MARCO — **Map 1.2:** Basilica di San Marco.

- Virgin's Family Tree
- Doge's banquet hall
- Pala d'Oro (extra €2 admission, paid inside)
- St Mark's sarcophagus
- Cupola of the Prophets
- Ascension Cupola
- Pentecost Cupola
- Last Judgement
- Dome of Genesis

The floors add to the spectacle, made of tessellated marble with geometric and animal designs.

Treasury

The *Tesoro* (treasury) is a buffet of religious relics of significance to Venice, as well as the spoils of the Crusades. Several of the Doges' remains have also been interred here.

Museum

The *Museo* (museum) name is slightly misleading in terms of the broader appeal that it has. You can you view amazing architectural drawings of the basilica dated from 13th to 16th centuries, and the museum is the only way to access some of the best views of the interior and onto Piazza San Marco.

Step outside onto the *Loggia dei Cavalli* balcony and look up to admire the reproductions of the 2nd century produced bronze four horses. Keeping with the theme of interior decoration through plunder, these magnificent statues made their way from Constantinople's (now Istanbul) hippodrome. Views across the piazza from here are some of the best elevated views to be had (second to the bell tower), although you will be jockeying with many others to drink it all in.

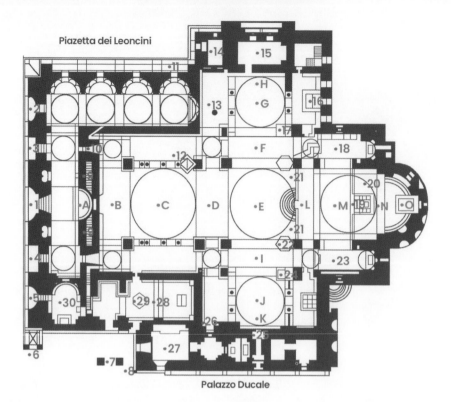

Piazetta dei Leoncini

Palazzo Ducale

Mosaics

A	Arch of Paradise	I	The Washing of the Feet, Temptation in the Wilderness
B	Arch of the Apocalypse	J	St. Leonard
C	Scenes of Pentecost	K	Four miracles of Jesus
D	Scenes from the Passion	L	St. Peter, The Resurrection, etc.
E	The Ascension	M	Choir mosaics
F	St. Michael with sword	N	Lamb of God
G	St. John	O	Christ in Majesty, with Saints
H	Mary's family tree		

Floor plan

1	Main portal	18	Capella di San Pietro
2-5	Portal recesses	19	High Altar
6	Piestra del Bando	20	Pala d'Oro
7	Pilastri Acritani	21	Iconostasis
8	Sculpture of the Tetrarchs	22	Reliquary
9	Museo Marciano stairway	23	Capella di San Clemente
10	Porta di San Pietro	24	Altare di San Giacomo
11	Porta dei Fiori	25	Palazzo Ducale
12	Capitello del Crocifisso	26	Entrance to the Treasury
13	Romanesque stoup with angels	27	Tesoro (Treasury)
14	Cappella della Madonna dei Mascoli	28	Battistero (Baptistry)
15	Capella di Saint'Isidro	29	Font dating from 1546 CE
16	Cappella della Madonna Nicopeia	30	Capella Zen d. 1501)
17	Altare di S Pietro		

Logistics

Location information

⊘ Piazza San Marco

⚓ San Marco

🌐 www.basilicasanmarco.it

#basilicasanmarco, #basilicadisanmarco, #stmarksbasilica

Tickets and opening times

🕐 09:45 – 17:00 Monday - Saturday.
14:00 – 17:00 Sunday (16:00 in Winter).

$ *Free*

▣ Just line up out the front of the Basilica.

"Skip the line" option

Entry to the Basilica itself is free, however you will need to wait in the long line to get in for most of the year. To combat this, you can purchase a "skip the line" ticket in advance for entry between April and the beginning of November.

$ €3

▣ www.venetoinside.com/attraction-tickets-in-veneto/tickets/skip-the-line-saint-marks-basilica/

This allows you to use the "Skip the line" entrance. As noted above, you'll need to purchase a separate ticket to access the Museum (purchase on site). If for nothing else, the price of admission to the Museum affords fantastic views directly across Piazza San Marco.

At high water times, the piazza and the basilica are prone to flooding. This may have an impact on your ability to access the site!

**24mm, f/11, ISO 100, 30 sec
FF camera**
1.13   A mild *acqua alta* provides an excellent reflective surface for long exposure shots.

Basilica museum

🕐 Basilica opening – 15 minutes before closing.

$ €5 / €2.50

🎫 Inside the Basilica, at the museum entrance.

Treasury

🕐 Basilica opening times.

$ €3

🎫 Inside the Basilica, at the treasury entrance.

Visit duration

Allow 30 minutes to an hour to absorb the interiors of the basilica, and an extra 30 minutes to an hour if you elect to visit the treasury and the museum (the latter is great for photo opportunities).

35mm, f/5.6, ISO 125, 1/500 sec
FF camera
1.14 Copper decorative pole outside of Basilica di San Marco.

Best time to visit

The beginning or end of opening hours are generally the least busy. The later in the afternoon, the greater the chances of having the place a little more to yourself. This can lead to more chances of getting photos without strangers wandering into frame.

Luggage / bags

No big items are allowed inside. Leave your luggage in nearby Ateneo San Basso located on Piazzetta dei Leoncini, in front of the Gate of Flowers.

Photo tips and tricks

Vantage points

There are many places that you can get photos of the façade of Basilica di San Marco:

Piazza San Marco - For dazzling (almost blinding) shots of the golden mosaics lit up, position yourself in Piazza San Marco around an hour to 90 minutes before sunset.

16mm, f/11, ISO 400, 0.4 sec
CF 1.5x camera

1.15 Basilica di San Marco's golden interior.

Torre dell'Orologio - Accessing the roof top provides elevated views of the mosaics on the façade, although they can be somewhat obscured by the arches. It is also possible to spy the frescos through the porthole windows on the lower levels.

Campanile di San Marco - The best place to take in the domed design of the basilica, and clearly see its close connection with neighbour Palazzo Ducale.

No photos inside?

Signs posted at the entrance state that photography and videography of the interior are forbidden, although policing of this policy is inconsistent.

16mm, f/11, ISO 400, 0.4 sec
CF 1.5x camera

1.16 The upper balconies provide a great vantage point of the decorated domes of the Basilica.

Campanile di San Marco

The Campanile di San Marco (bell tower) is one of the most iconic architectural features of Venice and has inspired many replicas (and imitators) around the world. The bell tower has been nicknamed by residents as "El paròn de casa" (the landlord) – its looming presence can be seen throughout the city. Galileo Galilei even used the tower to demonstrate his telescope to the Doge of Venice in 1609, and there's a plaque in the viewing area to commemorate the occasion.

Architecture and layout

Built as an accompaniment to St Mark's Basilica (typical for Italian Catholic architecture), it was initially built in the 12th century as a lighthouse / watch tower for the port area immediately around the Basilica and Doge's Palace. The belfry was a 16th century addition. Over time, the 98.6m bell tower has been partially or completely destroyed several times. It has been fully rebuilt twice, from its initial construction in the 9th century to its latest rebuild in 1912.

Being the tallest structure in the Venetian lagoon, the bell tower was subject to repeated lightning strikes over its years. It was finally fitted with a lightning rod in 1776 CE which reduced the number of structural issues. The five bells in the tower signified different events in the city: the beginning and end of the working day (*Marangona*), midday (*Nona*), session of the Senate (*Mezza Terza*), a call for council meetings (*Maggior Consiglio*)and more ominously, executions (*Maleficio*).

© OPENSTREETMAP CONTRIBUTORS

PIAZZA SAN MARCO Map 1.3: Campanile di San Marco.

Above the belfry are two alternating symbols of Venice, the lion and the lady Justice. Above the pyramid is an embossed copper statue of the Archangel Gabriel. The statue acts as a wind vane, keeping with the maritime traditions of the city.

Logistics

Location information

⊘ Piazza San Marco

⚓ San Marco

🌐 www.basilicasanmarco.it/basilica/campanile/?lang=en

\# #campaniledisanmarco, #campanilesanmarco

Tickets and opening times

🕐 1st Nov to 31st Mar - 09:30 - 17:30.
1st to 15th Apr - 09:00 - 17:30.
16th Apr to 31st Oct - 09:30 - 21:00.

$ €8 / €4

Tickets are purchased at the front entrance at the base of the tower.

"Skip the line" option

$ €13 / €9 (includes entry)

www.venetoinside.com/attraction-tickets-in-veneto/tickets/st-marks-bell-towerskip-the-line-entry/

Visit duration

Allow 1-2 hours for your visit. This includes the initial time to get up to the observation level (there is one functioning elevator) and the line at the end to get back down.

Best time to visit

Accept that you won't get the observation deck to yourself, however if you are patient, spots with great views open up fairly frequently.

1.18 24mm, f/11, ISO 100, 30 sec
FF camera
Long exposure at "blue hour" (after sunset) looking out from the *campanile* at the lagoon.

Tip

Purchase your ticket to enter the tower an hour before sunset. There is no restriction (as such) on how long you can be up there, and eventually the security guards will usher you back down to the ground. You'll no doubt be sharing the last elevator ride back down with fellow photographers!

█ Photo tips and tricks

Vantage points

Being the tallest structure in Venice, the bell tower acts as a useful navigational aide throughout the city. As such, you can get photos of the top section of the bell tower from many places. However, for views of the whole building here are the best places to position yourself:

Piazza San Marco - If you want a crowd-free view, refer to photographing Piazza San Marco (page 20).

Torre dell'Orologio - Views from both the roof and through the lower level portholes provide a more "mid-height" photo of the entire tower.

Basilica di San Marco - The balcony of the basilica provides an elevated view of the tower. Break out your widestangle lens.

Palazzo Ducale - Look for the views from the *loggia* (covered balconies), included as part of the Secret Itineraries tours (page 44). The tower is visible from the prison cells on the lower levels; a further reminder to those incarcerated.

Basilica di San Giorgio Maggiore - Stand outside of the basilica, just as you exit the *vaporetto* service, and face Piazza San Marco. The view includes the bell tower as well as other key landmarks of the piazza. Best views are in the morning (with the Eastern sun) using a decent telephoto lens to bridge the distance.

Photo opportunities to consider

Sunrise - Head towards the lagoon near Palazzo Ducale and look back East. The tower is the first building to be kissed by the sunrise.

Sunset - The early evening (around an hour before sunset) is the best time to capture most of the sun on the bell tower from the piazza. Bear in mind that the lower half of the tower will be in shadow when the sun falls below the height of the buildings on the West side of the piazza.

 16mm, f/11, ISO 100, 1/320 sec
CF 1.5x camera

1.19 *Campanile* view from the Basilica balcony.

Wide-angle - There are few vantage points that you'll be able to capture the entire tower with a regular zoom lens. Shooting with a wide-angle lens opens up possibilities from different directions facing the tower. Ideally, try to include people to give scale.

 75mm, f/5.6, ISO 400, 1/250 sec
FF camera

1.20 Decorative gates at the *campanile* entrance.

Portrait mode - Portrait mode with a regular zoom can often capture the full height of the tower from towards the rear (West side) of the piazza.

Arches as frames - The numerous arches of the *Procuratie Vecchie* (Old Procuracies) act as great frames for photos of the tower and basilica.

70mm, f/5.6, ISO 500, 1/250 sec
FF camera

1.21   The winged lion of St Mark decorated outside the *campanile*.

Advanced tip

Weather can be fickle, no matter where you travel. There is limited appeal to photos from the top of the tower on a cloudy or rainy day. If you have the ability to be flexible with your schedule, and ideally are visiting the tower alone, look to purchase the "skip the line" ticket on the intended day of visit so you can take advantage of good weather (or avoid the bad). You'll need to have the order confirmation email on your phone to show the ticket inspector. This strategy comes with a small degree of risk that all tickets could get sold out before the day, and usually tickets for the sunset period are the first to go.

70mm, f/8, ISO 100, 1/500 sec
FF camera

1.22   Viewing the *campanile* from the South West corner of Palazzo Ducale.

 1.23
24mm, f/8, ISO 200, 10 sec
FF camera
Long exposure at "blue hour" (after sunset) looking out from the *campanile* at the lagoon.

 1.24
24mm, f/11, ISO 200, 20 sec
FF camera
Long-exposure during "blue hour", using a normal zoom lens to capture the *campanile*.

50mm, f/8, ISO 100, 1/200 sec
CF 1.5x camera
Close-up view of the clock face from the balcony
of the nearby Basilica.

Torre dell'Orologio

The Torre dell'Orologio (clock tower), impressive in its own right, has to compete for attention in Piazza San Marco! Originally built in the 15th century, the clock was intended to flaunt the riches of Venice, and perhaps to serve as an actual clock. It is positioned such that it is visible from the Venetian lagoon, useful to help mariners with navigation and planning.

Architecture and layout

The Torre dell'Orologio is a 500-year old wonder built by the architect Mauro Codussi. There are many features of the tower that can be missed on initial inspection, each described below (moving from bottom to top).

Archway - Something a little less obvious is that the clock tower serves as the entrance way to the streets (*Merceria*) that navigate towards the market centre of Venice in Rialto.

Side buildings - There are two side buildings to the clock tower, which have been let out as retail space since the 18th century.

Main clock face - Decorated in rich blue and gold, this operates as a 24-hour clock (sporting Roman numerals). This is an astrological clock with the sun, moon, and the 12 signs of the zodiac all represented and moving in appropriate time. The Earth is represented as the small sphere in the centre of the clock.

Second clock - Often missed as it is somewhat hidden in the shadows, there is also clock on rear side of the tower. This clock is a more simplistic style, and without the astrological adornments.

PIAZZA SAN MARCO | Map 1.4: Torre dell'Orologio. | © OPENSTREETMAP CONTRIBUTORS

Virgin and Child - This balcony level has two sets of numbers: the left-hand side is the hour of the day in Roman numerals, and the right-hand side is minutes (in five-minute intervals) using Arabic numerals.

Lion of St Mark - The winged lion heraldic symbol holding a Bible represents Venice. The Bible is inscribed with *"Pax tibi Marce, evangelista meus"* (May Peace be with you, Mark, my evangelist).

Moors of Venice - Two bronze statues on the top of the tower of an older and younger man are known as the Moors (Mori). The name stems from their original dark appearance from the bronze on the statues, a rather crude reference to the Moors from the Southern Mediterranean. The two statues are said to represent the passage of time, and hence "ring" the bell with a single sequence to mark the hour.

Logistics

Location information

⊘ Piazza San Marco

⚓ San Marco

🌐 torreorologio.visitmuve.it/en/home/

\# #torreorologio, #torredellorologio

Tickets and opening times

All visits must be booked online in advance.

All tours are with an Englishspeaking guide.

🕐 Monday to Wednesday: 11:00 and 12:00.
Thursday to Sunday: 14:00 and 15:00.

\$ €8 / €4

🎟 muve.vivaticket.it/eng/tour/torre-dellorologio/567

Visit duration

Tours last 90 minutes.

16mm, f/6.3, ISO 400, 1/25 sec
CF 1.5x camera
1.26
The three *magi* (wise men) that are used for two Catholic special occasions each year.

Best time to visit

As above, you have to book in advance to join a guided tour.

▍Photo tips and tricks

Vantage points

There are many places that you can to get great photos of the clock tower, including:

Piazza di San Marco - Stand out the front of the main entrance of the bell tower to give yourself sufficient distance to get a full view of the clock face.

Merceria - As you are following the street on your way to Piazza San Marco, don't forget to look up! Given that the clock is somewhat hemmed in by surrounding buildings, middle of the day is your best chance at decent light.

Basilica di San Marco - The balcony of the basilica provides an elevated view of the clock tower and brings you level with the main clock face.

Campanile di San Marco - This is the best vantage point to get a shot of Moors ringing the bell.

Basilica di San Giorgio Maggiore - Stand outside of the basilica, just as you exit the *vaporetto* service, and face Piazza San Marco. This almost dead-on view looks straight through the two columns to the clock tower. Best views are in the morning (with the Eastern sun) using a decent telephoto lens.

Photo opportunities to consider

Best light - The clock face is nicely illuminated by the sun around 2-4 hours after sunrise. Shadows will be cast from the West over the clock face into the afternoon and evening.

Special occasions - For two Catholic observances each year, Epiphany (6 January) and Ascension Day (linked to Easter), the three *Magi* (wise men) appear and bow to the Virgin and Child and then disappear. The purpose of the balcony is to support this procession.

 16mm, f/3.5, ISO 400, 1/20 sec
CF 1.5x camera
1.27 Mechanical workings of the clock five-minute intervals (left) and hours (right).

 28mm, f/11, ISO 1600, 1/160 sec
FF camera
1.29 The semi-hidden rear clock face of Torre dell'Orologio visible from the *Merceria*.

 16mm, f/11, ISO 100, 1/320 sec
FF camera
1.28 The two "Moors" ringing the bell on top of Torre dell'Orologio clock tower.

30mm, f/8, ISO 100, 1/320 sec
FF camera

1.30   Scala dei Giganti with giant statues of Mars and Neptune greeting visitors.

Palazzo Ducale

The government and official residence of the Doges (similar to a Duke) of Venice since 1340 CE, the Palazzo Ducale (Doge's Palace) is one of the "must see" locations in Venice. The palace is great for anyone who wants to deepen their understanding of the historical, cultural and political importance of Venice This is a building that until 1797 CE has followed the developments of the millennial Republic of Venice (Palazzo Ducale was the seat of the Doge of Venice).

It remained the seat of power up to 1797 when Napoleon took over the city, ending the 1100 years of Ducal rule of the city. Then came the Habsburgs under Austrian rule. Finally, annexation in 1866 brought Venice into the Italian fold.

Architecture and layout

This Gothic masterpiece has undergone three construction phases during its life, with each level adding to the architectural beauty it is now. White Istrian stone and Veronese red marble are the key building materials that provide the palace with its distinct colours. The wing facing St. Mark's basin (i.e. the lagoon) is the oldest part of the building, last rebuilt in 1340 CE.

The wing facing onto Piazza San Marco was constructed in 1424, and the the wing facing the small *Rio de la Canonica o de Palazzo* canal was built between 1483 and 1565. The buildings are a great example of the Venetian Gothic architectural style, with some nods to other styles along the way.

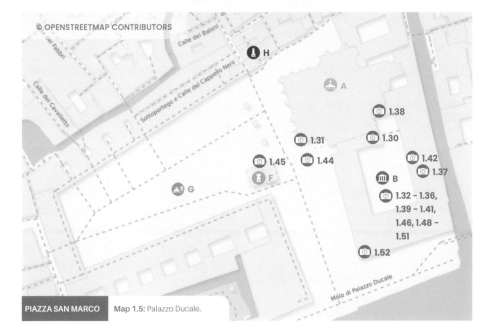

PIAZZA SAN MARCO   Map 1.5: Palazzo Ducale.

Some of the key features and places to visit:

Courtyard - As you enter the palace, you are greeted by a giant cauldron. From here, you can see how interconnected the palace was with the neighbouring basilica.

Scala dei Giganti - This rather grand staircase was constructed in 1485 CE by Antonio Rizzo. In 1567, Sansovino was commissioned to create the statues of Mars and Neptune that stand guard over the top of the staircase.

Museo dell'Opera - Owing to continued maintenance, or overhaul courtesy of the many fires that swept through, a dedicated office was built to oversee such efforts. Nowadays this space is used for displaying remnants of the earlier eras of the palace.

Doge's apartments - A blend of the private residence of the Doge (an elected position) and public spaces for the Ducal advisors and receiving guests. There are several pieces of iconic Venetian artwork on display, including works by Titian, Tullio, and Lombardo. The Sala dello Scudo (reference to the coat-of-arms of the incumbent Doge) room contains maps of the world as understood by the Venetians.

Scala d'Oro (Golden staircase) - The name says it all, really! The 24-carat gold stuccowork design is something to behold, and even the small paintings on the ceiling have some intrigue. A large amount of patience is required to get photos with few people in the room. The best bet is to visit at the end of opening hours.

Scala delle Quattro Porte (Hall of the Four Doors) - More of a gateway to other rooms, there are several important pieces by Titian, Cambi, and Tiepolo to admire. Antecollegio (Council antechamber) - Important guests waited here before their audience with members of the Senate. This was naturally a chance for expectation management, with pieces by Tintoretto and Veronese containing allegorical references to the Venetian republic's place in the world.

Collegio (Council chamber) - Once making their way from the antecollegio, important guests were received by the Senate here. In addition, the Senate conducted important foreign and domestic affairs from here. Sala del Senato (Senate chamber) - The private space for the Senate to oversee affairs of the state.

Sala Consiglio dei Dieci (Chamber of the Council of Ten) - Named after a 1310 CE plot to overthrow the government. Here anonymous accusations against the state were reviewed.

Sala del Maggior Consiglio (Grand Council chamber) - This huge hall, at 53m by 25m, is still one of the largest rooms in Europe! This is where the Great Council met, an egalitarian representation of Venetian families. Linger here to admire the huge works, including a 22m by 7m by Tintoretto and the ceiling piece by Veronese.

New prisons - Built in the newer part of the palace in the 16th century, it was intended to provide more humane cells for prisoners.

Bridge of Sighs - The enclosed bridge that links the two sections of the palace over the canal. The name derives from the supposed sighs let out by prisoners on their way to jail – this was their last real glimpse of Venice and the lagoon, through the small porthole windows.

Armoury - Contains a large collection of weapons, armour, spoils of battle, and torture devices.

50mm, f/8, ISO 100, 1/500 sec
FF camera

1.31 Close-up of the Venetian Gothic facades of Palazzo Ducale from the Basilica balcony.

Ground floor

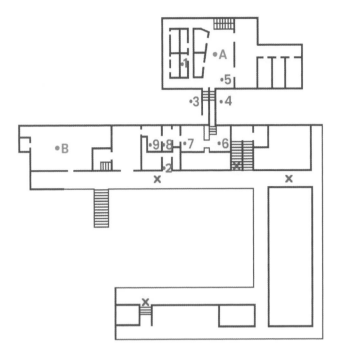

Prisons and institutional rooms

1	*Loggias* (Logge)	7	Sala dell'Avogaria (The Chamber of State Advocacies)
2	Scala d'Oro (Golden staircase)	8	Sala dello Scrigno ("Scrigno" Room)
3	Entrance to the prisons (prigioni)	9	Sala della Milizia da Mar (The Chamber of the Navy)
4	Ponte dei Sospiri (Bridge of Sighs)	A	Prisons (Prigioni)
5	Prisons (Prigioni)	B	Offices (not accessible)
6	Sala dei Censori (The Chamber of Censors)		

Courtyard

1	Museo dell'Opera	A	Museo dell'Opera
2	Cortile (Courtyard)	B	Scala dei Censori (Stair of the Censors)
3	Museum Areas currently not open to the public		

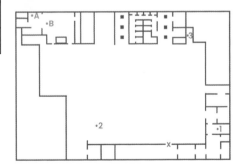

Pozzi (wells) - The water-level prisons, where it doesn't take much imagination to realise the damp squalor that prisons suffered here.

Chamber of the Secret Chancellery - Sitting in this chamber, whilst fairly understated, has a real sense of history, and you can sense the power that was held over the citizens of Venice from this room.

First floor

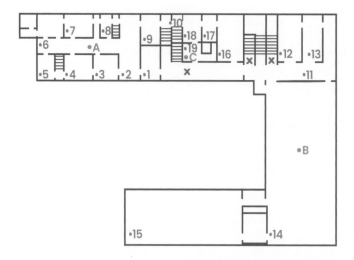

First floor institutional rooms

1	Sala degli Scarlatti (Scarlet Room)	12	Sala della Quarantia Civil Vecchia (Chamber of Quarantia Civil Vecchia)
2	Sala dello Scudo (Shield Room)	13	Sala dei Guariento (Guariento Room)
3	Sala Grimani (Grimani Room)	14	Sala dei Maggior Consiglio (Chamber of the Great Council)
4	Sala Erizzo (Erizzo Room)	15	Sala dello Scrutinio (Chamber of Scrutiny)
5	Sala degli Stucchi o Priuli (Stucco Room)	16	Sala della Quarantia Criminale (The Chamber of appeals court)
6	Sala dei Filosofi (Philosophers Room)	17	Sala dei Cuoi (Cuoi Room)
7	Sala Corner (Corner Room)	18	Sala dei Magistrato alle Leggi (Chamber of the three Magistrates)
8	Sala dei Ritratti (Portraits Room)	A	Doge's apartments
9	Sala degli Scudieri (The Equerries Room)	B	Institutional Rooms
10	Scala d'Oro (Golden staircase)	C	Prisons (entrance)
11	Liagò		

24mm, f/5.6, ISO 640, 1/60 sec
FF camera

1.32 The opulent Scala d'Oro (Golden staircase).

Second floor

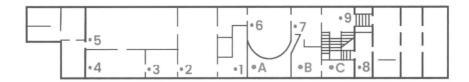

Second floor institutional rooms

1	Atrio Quadrato (Square Atrium)	7	Sala della Bussola (Compass Room)
2	Sala delle Quattro Porte (Hall of the Four Doors)	8	Armeria (Armoury)
3	Sala dell'Anticollegio (Council antechambers)	9	Scala dei Censori (Censors Room)
4	Sala del Collegio (Council Chamber)	A	Stanze del Notaio Ducale (Room of the Ducal Notary)
5	Sala del Senato (Senate Chamber)	B	Sala dei Tre Capi (Chamber of the Three Head Magistrates)
6	Sala del Consiglio dei Dieci (Chamber of the Council of Ten)	C	Sala degli Inquisitori (Chamber of the Inquisitors)

24mm, f/5.6, ISO 1600, 1/20 sec
FF camera

1.33   Chamber of the Secret Chancellery.

24mm, f/11, ISO 100, 1.6 sec
FF camera

1.34   Sala del Maggior Consiglio (Grand Council Chamber), taking a long-exposure shot.

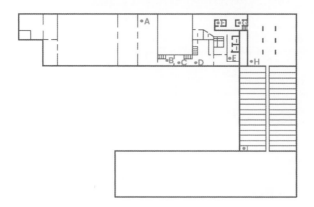

Special Itineraries:
Secret itineraries tour

A	Cancelleria Superiore (Superior Chancellor office)	F	Seconda cella di Casanova (Casanova's second cell)
B	Sala del ViceReggente (Room of the Vice-ruler)	G	Piombi (Prison cells)
C	Sala del Reggente (Room of the Ruler)	H	Sala d'Armi (Room of weapons)
D	Sala della Tortura (Torture Chamber)	I	Soffitto della Sala del Maggior Consiglio (Ceiling of the Room of the Great Council)
E	Prima cella di Casanova (Casanova's first cell)		

Chamber of torment - The name conjures up all sorts of ghastly deeds, as does the long rope hanging from the rafters in the centre of the room. This is where judges watched prisoners strung by their arms (behind their back) using the rope to get a confession.

Piombo (Old prisons) - The name stems from lead roof above the prison (a reference to the Latin *plumbum*). The cells held prisons of the Council of Ten (see above) and

28mm, f/8, ISO 100, 4 sec
FF camera
1.36 The entry to the Doge's apartment is framed by *St Christopher* by Titian.

24mm, f/11, ISO 100, 1.6 sec
FF camera
1.35 Ceiling of the Chambers of the Three Head Magistrates.

housed such luminaries as Casanova (who actually escaped!).

Chamber of the Inquisitors - Home of the feared magistrates that were charged with protecting state secrets.

Chamber of the Three Head Magistrates - A rotating role bestowed on members of the Council of Ten, to ensure that the courts were run efficiently. The octagonal piece by Zelotti, Victory of Virtue over Vice, seems to be a perfect decorative fit for the work of the room. There is a secret passage that leads from here back to the Chamber of the Council of Ten (see above).

Special Itineraries: The Doge's hidden treasures

This tour provides access to some of the treasures (particularly the artwork) that the Doges got to admire each day. This tour is also great for getting outdoor photos of the Basilica and elevated views of Piazza San Marco. Key highlights of the tour:

Porta della Carta - The official entrance to the palace during its time of operation, the exterior view (seen from the Piazza) is actually the best side to photograph.

Loggiato (covered balconies) - The Doge would emerge here to engage with the public during festivities. The views over Piazza San Marco and the lagoon are some of the best to be had.

Loggia Foscara - The continuation of the covered balcony provides a view in over the palace courtyard.

Hanging terrace - This terrace is hidden from public and provides close up views of one of the giant gothic windows of the Basilica.

Doge's apartment - Several treasures are on display here, often the worldly possessions of

35mm, f/8, ISO 100, 1/125 sec
FF camera
1.37 The *loggia* where the Doge would appear to interact with the crowds on the Piazza.

nuns who had come from wealthy families. The Doge had the excellent St Christopher by Titian to admire above the stairs leading out of his apartment.

Scala dei Giganti (Giant's Staircase) - The tour passes the staircase from an elevated position. Chiesetta - The brightly-lit private church of the Doge.

Antichiesetta - The "main" entrance to the Doge's private church, leading back to the rest of the palace.

Logistics

Location information

- ◎ Piazza San Marco
- ⚓ San Marco
- 🌐 palazzoducale.visitmuve.it/en/home/
- ◎ @palazzoducalevenezia

\# #palazzoducale, #palazzoducalevenezia, #dogespalace, #dogespalacevenice

Tickets and opening times

Entry to the Doge's Palace is along the side of the building off Piazza San Marco that faces onto the lagoon. There are separate lines for individuals ("walk ups"), groups, those with online bookings.

🕐 1st November to 31st March - 08:30 - 17:30 (last admission 16:30).
1st April to 31st October - 08:30 - 19:00 (last admission 18:00).

$ €20 / €13 (includes entry to Museo Correr, Museo Archeologico Nazionale and Monumental Rooms of the Biblioteca Nazionale Marciana).

24mm, f/8, ISO 100, 1/400 sec
FF camera
1.38 View from the hanging terrace on the way to the Doge's apartment.

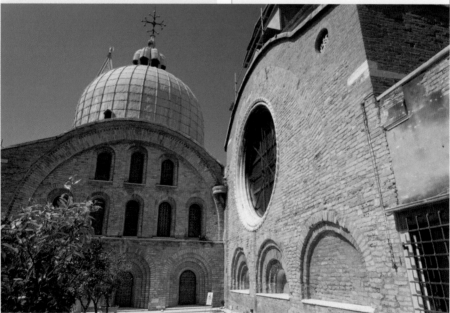

"Skip the line" option

A strong suggestion is to purchase your entry ticket online ahead of time so that you can skip the long queue.

$ €24.50 / €18.50 (includes entry to Museo Correr, Museo Archeologico Nazionale and Monumental Rooms of the Biblioteca Nazionale Marciana).

▭ palazzoducale.visitmuve.it/en/pianifica-la-tua-visita/bookings/

Use the same entry as above; however, use the (short) online bookings line. Make sure you have your email booking confirmation handy (on your phone or print out) to show. Once you're let inside proceed to the ticket office (on the left) to convert your booking into a ticket.

24mm, f/4, ISO 1600, 1/60 sec
FF camera
1.40 Articles on display in the State Treasures.

24mm, f/5.6, ISO 1600, 1/40 sec
FF camera
1.39 Ceiling frescos in the Antichiesetta, portraying the death of St Mark.

Special itineraries tours

You'll need to purchase your ticket in advance, the further in advance the better. Both tours last approximately 90 minutes.

🕐 Secret itineraries tour - 09:55, 10:45, and 11:35 (daily).
Hidden Doge's treasure tour - 11:45 (daily).

💲 €20 / €14 (includes entry to Palazzo Ducale).

Secret itineraries tour - muve.vivaticket.it/index.php?nvpg[festivaldetail]

🎫 Hidden Doge's treasure tour - muve.vivaticket.it/eng/event/the-doge-s-hiddentreasures-english/70714

Use the same entry as above however use the (very short) special itineraries tour line. Make sure you have your email booking confirmation handy (on your phone or print out) to show. Once you're let inside proceed to the ticket office (on the left) to convert your booking into an actual ticket.

Visit duration

Even if you have little interest in the history or culture of Venice in its heyday, allow a minimum of two hours to explore the palace. For many sections, there are no easy ways to leave, and so you'll have to traverse 10 or so halls in order to find the nearest exit!

For those intrigued with any of the descriptions above (which are a very brief taster to what's in store), allow a minimum of a half day.

Best time to visit

Visiting towards the end of the day is ideal, as most tour groups have moved through and have been herded off elsewhere.

Tip

If you don't have an interest in visiting the other museums, consider booking one of the Special Itineraries tours (see below) instead. These tickets are cheaper than the general admission, include access to Palazzo Ducale, and come with a special tour that most people miss out on. And... you get to use the "special itineraries" entry line, which is the shortest line of them all!

Luggage / bags

Anything above the size of a hand bag / small personal bag is not allowed to be taken into the Doge's palace buildings (although they're fine in the courtyard). There is a free cloak / bag room inside the Palace off to the right (East side) of the courtyard. Note that the staff are pretty strict on enforcing the "no bags in the halls" rule.

▌Photo tips and tricks

Vantage points

There are many places that you can to get great exterior photos, including:

24mm, f/4, ISO 3200, 1/30 sec
FF camera
1.41 Piombi (prison) cells.

24mm, f/8, ISO 100, 1/200 sec
FF camera

1.42 Looking out from the state rooms of Palazzo Ducale.

Piazza di San Marco - Key features to capture include the Porta della Carta entrance, the covered arches (taken from inside), as well as the details on the columns on the upper floors.

Basilica di San Marco - The balcony of the basilica provides an elevated view of the colonnaded *loggia* on the upper floors.

Campanile di San Marco - Great perspectives of the exterior walls facing into the piazza as well as the reminder of how interwoven the palace and the Basilica were.

Basilica di San Giorgio Maggiore - Stand outside of the basilica, just as you exit the *vaporetto* service, and face Piazza San Marco – it's all there!

Punta della Dogana - This oblique angle of the palace, with the gondolas anchored by the shore, gives a real sense of how merchants arrived in the city in centuries past.

Photo opportunities to consider

Many of the points for Piazza San Marco (page 20) apply here. The tips below are specific to the interior:

Patience - Unfortunately, Palazzo Ducale wasn't exactly designed to move large number of tour groups through its midst with any degree of efficiency. If you wait for a few minutes, and take several shots in the process, you can usually get a people-free photo of almost any part of the palace. And if not, there are techniques in Photoshop to remove people out of the image!

Wide-angle lens - If you are forced to choose one lens for your visit, consider bringing your wide-angle lens. It will work well in the often low-light environments inside, as well as allow you to capture the

 90mm, f/11, ISO 1600, 1/250 sec
FF camera
1.44 Porta della Carta, the *palazzo's* real entrance.

expansive frescos and majesty of many of the rooms. Some of the rooms are even lined with benches / shelves that could be used as an impromptu base to take longer-exposure shots (this can blur / remove people wandering about).

Low-light - The prisons (basement levels) are very dark necessitating high ISO or wide apertures.

Outside views - Keep an eye out for views out windows onto Piazza San Marco from palace rooms. In addition, don't forget to pause on the Bridge of Sighs and capture the canal and lagoon. The same applies for the prison cell windows.

 24mm, f/4.5, ISO 3200, 1/15 sec
FF camera
1.49 The infamous Chamber of Torment, seen during the Secret Itineraries tour of Palazzo Ducale (Doge's palace).

 24mm, f/11, ISO 800, 1/320 sec
FF camera
1.45 Looking out over Piazza Ducale at sunset from the nearby *campanile*.

 24mm, f/5.6, ISO 640, 1/60 sec
FF camera
1.46 The opulent Scala d'Oro (Golden staircase).

 24mm, f/11, ISO 250, 1/40 sec
FF camera

1.47 Early morning in Piazza San Marco.

 40mm, f/8, ISO 100, 1/320 sec
CF 1.5x camera

1.43 Clock tower view from the Basilica balcony.

 24mm, f/5.6, ISO 3200, 1/20 sec
FF camera

1.48 Piombi (prison) cells.

 24mm, f/5.6, ISO 1000, 1/60 sec
FF camera
1.50 Chiesetta, the Doge's private church.

 56mm, f/5.6, ISO 400, 1/15 sec
CF 1.5x camera
1.51 Entrance to the basement prison cells.

2.00   45mm, f/11, ISO 125, 1/60 sec FF camera   You won't need to wait very long for several Venetian cliches to come together in one photo.

Bridges of Venice

A section of this sub-guide is dedicated to bridges, such is their importance to the city of Venice. They are the life blood for foot traffic for both locals and tourists. They range from the eponymous Rialto bridge, the largest over the Grand Canal all the way down to the tiny private bridges that connect to individual houses. The two banks of the Grand Canal are connected by four main bridges – Ponte di Rialto, Ponte dell'Accademia, Ponte della Costituzione, and Ponte degli Scalzi. One of the many names that Venice has collected over the years is the "City of Bridges", and the stats are clear:

- 391 bridges in Venice
- 12 bridges in Giudecca
- 72 private bridges (included in the 403 total)
- 150 canals
- 118 islands

The first bridges in Venice were flat wooden structures so that horses could move loads from one island to another. Over the centuries this has evolved, and in the 16th century the first arched stone bridges started appearing. The purpose of the stone arch was to allow boats to pass by unhindered.

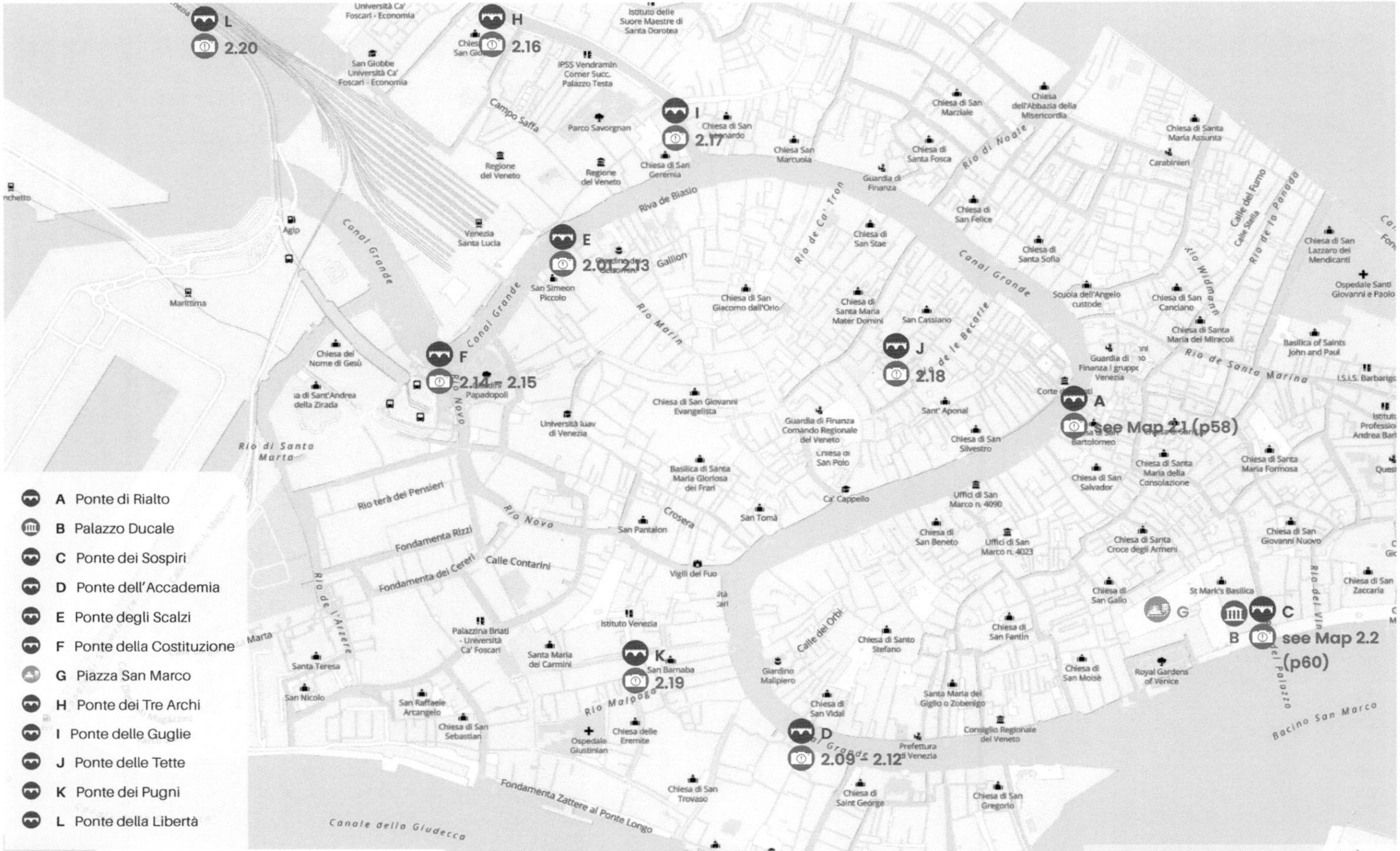

A Ponte di Rialto
B Palazzo Ducale
C Ponte dei Sospiri
D Ponte dell'Accademia
E Ponte degli Scalzi
F Ponte della Costituzione
G Piazza San Marco
H Ponte dei Tre Archi
I Ponte delle Guglie
J Ponte delle Tette
K Ponte dei Pugni
L Ponte della Libertà

BRIDGES Map 2.0: The major and historic bridges of Venice.

© OPENSTREETMAP CONTRIBUTORS

80mm, f/11, ISO 320, 1/250 sec
FF camera

2.01 Sunset across Ponte degli Scalzi.

45mm, f/11, ISO 640, 1/50 sec
FF camera

2.03 The Rialto bridge is almost empty at sunrise.

Being a densely populated city, the risk of fire was ever-present and so a desire to move away from wooden structures would (in theory) reduce the fire danger of the city. Today it is not uncommon to see locals with purpose-built trolleys, great for traversing bridges, sharing the footpath space with tourists. In addition to helping get from A to B, a bridge (and site of other bridges) can be a useful navigational aid when trying to find your place on the map.

55mm, f/11, ISO 50, 10 sec
FF camera

2.02 Enjoy watching the sunset from Rialto bridge, although you'll need to jostle for space.

Ponte di Rialto

No trip to Venice is complete without traversing the Rialto at least once. The most famous of the four bridges that span the Grand Canal, it is heavily trafficked during the day. It connects the San Polo and San Marco *sestieri* (districts), so is a useful thoroughfare for locals and tourists alike. First built in 1181 CE, tradition has it that was initially made with wooden poles. Its original name was Ponte della Moneta – a mint (coin production) was once on the San Marco banks near the bridge. Over the centuries, it was replaced by a structural wooden bridge, and the name was changed the current name. *Rialto* is a reference to the fact that the bridge passes high over the river. The current bridge opened for business in 1591 CE to much speculation that it wouldn't last long (predecessors had a long history of collapse for various reasons). It remained the only foot bridge over the Grand Canal for another

2.04 28mm, f/8, ISO 100, 1/160 sec
FF camera
Sunrise on the "quiet" North East side of the Rialto bridge.

three hundred years. The bridge formed part of the *Merceria* path connecting Piazza San Marco with the Rialto market (page 98).

Logistics

Location information

  Rialto

\# #rialtobridge, #rialtobridgevenice, #pontedirialto

Beat the crowd

A bit of patience is required when crossing the bridge during the day - there are a LOT of people. Stick to the centre section if you are not stopping to admire the view.

© OPENSTREETMAP CONTRIBUTORS

BRIDGES | **Map 2.1:** Ponte di Rialto.

Like most of Venice, you can have the bridge virtually to yourself before 7:00, and then again late in the night.

Photo tips and tricks

Long-exposure, no tripod

You can get great long exposure shots facing west by using the solid side barrier of the bridge to rest your camera (instead of needing a tripod). This requires a bit of patience and potentially having to jostle with the MANY other tourists. Make sure you carry a shutter release or remote control to help with long exposures.

Vantage points

View from the canal - You can capture the late afternoon sun on the bridge by catching a *vaporetto* heading West. Make sure you position yourself towards the front of the boat, or at the side where you can angle your camera out. Set your camera to Shutter priority, and set the shutter speed at a high value such as 1/500 sec. This helps counteract the motion of the boat, and the inevitable shakiness from holding your camera at a precarious angle. Also set your camera to continuous burst mode to increase the chances of getting a decent in-focus shot.

Sunrise - There can be great light coming across onto the North side of the Grand Canal, however there's fairly minimal activity on the water at this time. Gondolas will be covered up with tarps and moored. You're more likely to find modern boats plying the waters, including those disposing of garbage.

Sunset - The lead up to sunset has good light along the South side of the Grand Canal, with plenty of activity on the water to photograph.

16mm, f/8, ISO 100, 1/100 sec
CF 1.5x camera
2.06 Making use of the open windows inside Palazzo Ducale to photograph the Ponte dei Sospiri.

35mm, f/11, ISO 100, 1/100 sec
CF 1.5x camera
2.05 Quiet early morning looking out over the Grand Canal from the Rialto bridge.

24mm, f/11, ISO 50, 20 sec
FF camera
2.07 Long-exposure shot of Ponte dei Sospiri with the decorative statues of Palazzo Ducale.

Ponte dei Sospiri

A historic, charming Baroque style bridge made of Istrian stone, Ponte dei Sospiri (Bridge of Sighs) was constructed in 1614 CE. The bridge was designed by the nephew of the designer of the Rialto bridge and connects the Prigioni Nuove (New Prison) to the interrogation and rooms of the Magistrates (the state inquisitors). The name was said to have originated from the fact that prisoners would get their last glimpse of Venice (particularly, San Giorgio Maggiore) before heading to the cells to rot.

Logistics

Location information

 San Marco

 #pontedeisospiri, #bridgeofsighs, #pontedeisospirivenezia

Inside view

Entry to the bridge is part of the general admission to the Palazzo Ducale (page 38). Parts of the bridge path are only accessible if you take the Secret Itineraries tour (page 44).

Photo tips and tricks

Vantage points

Ponte della Paglia - This bridge becomes very popular during the day as a thoroughfare between San Marco and Castello. It is also where tourists will stop and pose for photos. Best lighting is in the morning.

Fondamenta della Canonica - A photo from this bridge can capture the Bridge of Sighs as well as a view out towards San Giorgio Maggiore. Owing to the large buildings in the vicinity, the best light (with least shadows)

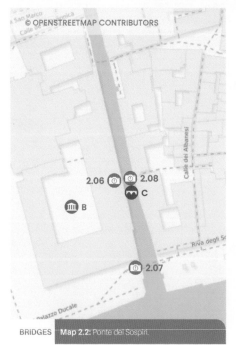

© OPENSTREETMAP CONTRIBUTORS

2.06   2.08

C

B

2.07

Map 2.2: Ponte dei Sospiri.

55mm, f/8, ISO 100, 1/160 sec
FF camera
2.08   Looking North through the stone windows of the Ponte dei Sospiri.

typically comes during the middle of the day.

Basilica di San Giorgio Maggiore - Stand outside of the basilica, just as you exit the *vaporetto* service, and face Piazza San Marco. The slightly oblique view is best in the morning (with the Eastern sun) using a decent telephoto lens to bridge the distance.

Views from the inside

Natural frames - The ornate window patterns are not large enough to squeeze through large diameter lenses, so photos are likely to include elements of the stone window. Use this in framing your shot – it helps tell the story of a prisoner's last view of the world.

Gondolas - The Rio di Palazzo that flows underneath the bridge is a prime spot for gondolas to pass by.

Lagoon views - Facing South provides a view of the bustle along Riva degli Schiavoni and San Giorgio Maggiore island.

2.09

45mm, f/11, ISO 100, 1/40 sec
FF camera
Using Ponte dell'Accademia to frame the sunrise and Chiesa di Santa Maria della Salute.

Ponte dell'Accademia

A bridge that is famous more for the views along the Grand Canal than the bridge design itself. Found at the Southernmost part of the city, the bridge spans the Grand Canal and serves as the connection between Piazza San Marco and Galleria dell'Accademia. The original construction of the bridge was supposed to be in 1488 CE. However, due to lack of funds, it was postponed until 1854. The original bridge was a metal design however it suffered the same backlash as Ponte degli Scalzi and was changed into a wooden bridge in the 1930s designed by Eugenio Miozzi. The bridge has only recently completed a multi-year refurbishment as of 2018, and so is now ready to be photographed without scaffolding after a long hiatus.

Logistics

⚓ Accademia

\# #pontedellaccademia

Beat the crowd

It is hard not to experience a trip to Venice without crossing this bridge at some point – it is the key connector to many significant parts of the city. As such, there are plenty of people that cross during the day and pause to take photos along both sides along the Grand Canal. The crowds die down during the evening.

Public toilet

There are toilet facilities on the West side of the bridge (€1.50 in coins).

40mm, f/11, ISO 50, 10 sec
FF camera

2.10 Standing on Ponte dell'Accademia capturing boat light trails at sunrise.

45mm, f/11, ISO 160, 1/160 sec
FF camera

2.12 The wooden Ponte dell'Accademia bridge has recently been reopened (late 2018).

Photo tips and tricks

Bouncy bouncy

The bridge is one of the best vantage points for sunrise photographs of Venice, in particular the dome of Chiesa di Santa Maria della Salute. However, the wooden bridge isn't as solid as other stone bridges in the city. This means that long-exposure shots can be tricky to obtain, particularly if people are walking around.

Your best bet is to increase shutter speed (and increase ISO), or shoot before sunrise.

55mm, f/11, ISO 100, 20 sec
FF camera

2.11 Long-exposure shot facing East down the Grand Canal at sunrise.

24mm, f/11, ISO 100, 117 sec
FF camera

2.13 Late evening long-exposure of the Grand Canal from Ponte degli Scalzi.

Additional famous bridges

| Ponte degli Scalzi

Constructed in 1858 under the Habsburg rule, it is one of the four bridges that span the Grand Canal. The name is thought to have derived from the order of bare-footed friars, known as Scalzi, whose monastery was the nearby Chiesa di Santa Maria di Nazareth (commonly called Chiesa degli Scalzi).

It was designed by the English engineer Alfred Neville and was the first Venetian bridge built using cast iron. However, it received a lot of criticism for not fitting with Venetian design aesthetic, leading to its stone reconstruction in 1934 headed by architect Eugenio Miozzi.

Beat the crowd

The Scalzi is the first bridge you'll come in contact with if you arrive at the Venice Santa Lucia *ferrovia* (railway station). Tourists are often seen man-handling their large luggage over the bridge during the day. This tends to not be an issue in the evening.

Logistics

 Ferrovia

 #pontedegliscalzi

Photo tips and tricks

The bridge is a solid construction, and the centre of the bridge can be used as a stable surface for long exposure photos. River-bound traffic tends to be mostly modern

70mm, f/11, ISO 500, 1/250 sec
FF camera
2.14 The bridge design has been criticised for being at odds with the "look" of the rest of Venice.

vessels, although gondolas can be seen during the day.

Ponte delle Costituzione

Also called the Calatrava bridge, the Ponte della Costituzione is the newest bridge in Venice. It was inaugurated in 2008 and is now the fourth bridge crossing the Grand Canal. It is often criticised for its shape as well as its low and far-reaching steps which many say (and feel) inconvenient for

walking. However, there are also those who welcomed it with great enthusiasm saying the structure does not contrast with the magical scenery of the lagoon.

Logistics

⚓ P. le Roma

\# #pontedellacostituzione

Photo tips and tricks

The red ribbed steel design of the bridge is best viewed from underneath, on the South West bank.

80mm, f/11, ISO 500, 1/250 sec
FF camera
2.15 The bright-red mobility capsules of Ponte delle Costituzione were retro-fitted after opening.

Ponte dei Tre Archi

Translated as the Bridge of Three Arches, it is unique of all the bridges in Venice because it is the only surviving three arch bridge. It is also one of the largest bridges in the city. Originally built in 1503 CE, it was originally named Ponte di San Giobbe, because of its proximity to the nearby church of the same name. The current design harks back to 1861.

Logistics

⚓ Tre Archi, Crea

\# #pontedeitrearchi

35mm, f/11, ISO 200, 1/250 sec
FF camera
2.16 One of the most elaborate bridges in Venice, Ponte dei Tre Archi is off the tourist trail.

Ponte delle Guglie

Also known as the "Bridge of Spires" due to the four slender *guglie* (obelisks) positioned at each of its corners. The stone and brick bridge was constructed in 1823, and has interesting carvings such as gargoyles on its surface. The East end of the bridge leads on to the market on Rio Terà S. Leonardo (page 175).

Logistics

⚓ Guglie

\# #pontedelleguglie

Ponte delle Tette

Translated into English as a vulgar variant of "Bridge of Breasts", the name came from the fact that the area was a sanctioned red-light district during the 16th century. It was not uncommon for prostitutes to show their breasts to entice potential customers. This red-light district was encouraged by official decree to help stem the perceived rise of homosexuality that was deemed to be a "social problem" at the time. In addition, taxes on prostitution were quite a lucrative way of helping fund some major works in the city during this period.

Logistics

⚓ S. Silvestro

\# #pontedelletette

Ponte dei Pugni

Translated as the Bridge of Fists, Ponte dei Pugni has an exciting history. A few hundred years ago, it hosted the so-called "War of the fists" between the Castellani and the Nicolloti districts. Each district had a champion who would box for hours on this bridge as people cheered from their windows. The victory move for the fighters was to throw their opponent into the water. The district that kept their men "dry" won the challenge.

The fights weren't necessarily restricted to fists too... it wasn't uncommon for attendees to bring knives, daggers, sticks, and even spiked boat poles. Clearly things didn't always end well!

2.17 45mm, f/8, ISO 100, 1/250 sec
FF camera
The distinct *guglie* (obelisks) that give Ponte delle Guglie its name.

2.18 24mm, f/11, ISO 400, 1/250 sec
FF camera
The former red-light district that included the then infamous Ponte delle Tette.

105mm, f/8, ISO 100, 1/125 sec
FF camera
2.19   Local residents relaxing by Ponte dei Pugni
towards the end of the day.

Logistics

⚓ Ca' Rezzonico

\# #pontedeipugni

4mm, f/2.2, ISO 25, 1/1600 sec
iPhone 6s (CF 7x) camera
2.20   Capturing Ponte della Libertà (Bridge of Liberty)
before landing at Venice airport.

Ponte della Libertà

Designed by engineer Miozzi in 1931, it connects Venice's city centre to the mainland. Benito Mussolini inaugurated it in 1933 and gave it the name "Ponte Littorio". After the end of the Second World War, the bridge was renamed "Liberty Bridge" in honour of Venice's liberation from the Nazis.

Logistics

⚓ P. le Roma

\# #pontedellaliberta

Photo tips and tricks

If arriving in Venice by air, flights will approach from the South. Make sure you book a seat on the right-hand side of the plane, and a seat that doesn't have its view obstructed by the wing or engine. And arrive during the day for best results!

Churches of Venice

Venice is a hub of churches, cathedrals, and basilicas that have been built, extended, improved, and sometimes cleared away over the ages. Depending on your method of counting, there are around 140 churches still standing in the Venetian lagoon. In addition, there are three non-Catholic churches, and seven synagogues. The styles of architecture of churches in Venice has evolved over the years, much like the city itself. Wealthy patrician families contributed significantly to their construction, partly to show their faith, and to demonstrate their economic power. There are several styles of construction, ranging from Baroque to Byzantine through to Neoclassical, many churches becoming masterpieces of design - some of the most plain-looking façade churches tend to have the most impressive displays inside.

Similar to churches all over Italy, Venetian churches have mostly opted to display their art in-situ rather than relocate the art to museums. A who's who of the Italian (and further afield) art world have pieces spread throughout the city which gives you the best chance to appreciate the works as the artists had intended.

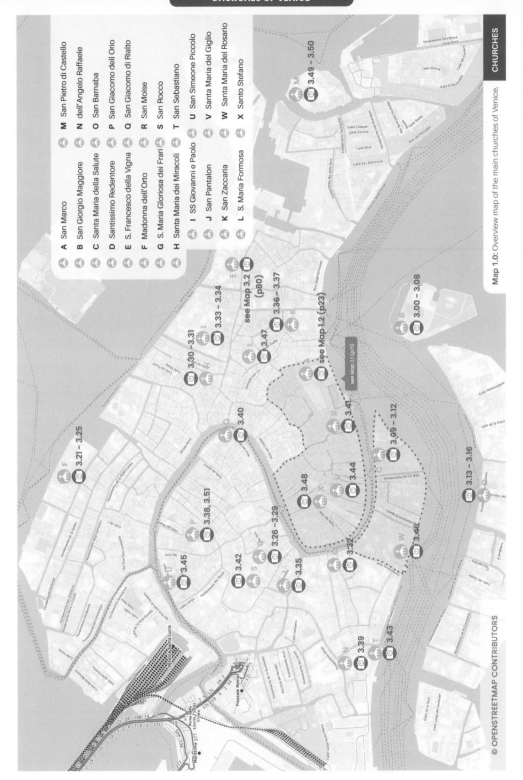

A San Marco
B San Giorgio Maggiore
C Santa Maria della Salute
D Santissimo Redentore
E S. Francesco della Vigna
F Madonna dell'Orto
G S. Maria Gloriosa dei Frari
H Santa Maria dei Miracoli
I SS Giovanni e Paolo
J San Pantalon
K San Zaccaria
L S. Maria Formosa
M San Pietro di Castello
N dell'Angelo Raffaele
O San Barnaba
P San Giacomo dell Orio
Q San Giacomo di Rialto
R San Moise
S San Rocco
T San Sebastiano
U San Simeone Piccolo
V Santa Maria del Giglio
W Santa Maria del Rosario
X Santo Stefano

CHURCHES

see Map 3.2 (p80)
see Map 1.2 (p23)
see Map 3.1 (p27)

3.49 – 3.50
3.00 – 3.08
3.33 – 3.34
3.36 – 3.37
3.47
3.30 – 3.31
3.21 – 3.25
3.40
3.99 – 3.12
3.41
3.13 – 3.16
3.38, 3.51
3.48
3.44
3.26 – 3.29
3.32
3.46
3.45
3.42
3.35
3.39
3.43

Map 1.0: Overview map of the main churches of Venice.

© OPENSTREETMAP CONTRIBUTORS

45mm, f/11, ISO 50, 25 sec
FF camera
3.01   Long-exposure shot of Basilica di San Giorgio Maggiore from the edge of Piazza San Marco.

Basilica di San Giorgio Maggiore

One of the most prominent churches in Venice, the structures started out as a monastery for Benedictine monks. The Renaissance-style basilica was designed in the 16th century by fabled architect Andrea Palladio and is a feast for the eyes both inside and out. The façade has majestic columns that support the central section of the church, while the interiors houses works of art by masters Ricci and Bassano. Two of the most prestigious residents of the basilica are Tintoretto's "Last Supper" and "Deposition of Christ".

Logistics

🌐 Isola di S. Giorgio Maggiore

⚓ S. Giorgio

🌐 en.turismovenezia.it/Venezia/Chiesa-di-San-Giorgio-Maggiore-6.05.html

\# #chiesadisangiorgiomaggiore, #isoladisangiorgiomaggiore #basilicadisangiorgiomaggiore

Tickets and opening times

🕐 1st April to 31st October - 09:30 to 19:00.
1st November to 31st March - 08:30 to 18:00.

Sunday visits – closed for mass between 10:40 and 12:00 (visitors welcome to join).

$ *Free*

Campanile

🕐 Same hours as the basilica. Last ascent to the bell tower is 20 minutes before closing time.

$ €6 / €4

🎟 Ticket office inside the basilica.

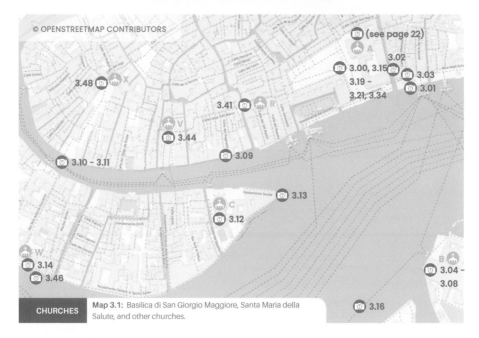

(see page 22)

CHURCHES **Map 3.1:** Basilica di San Giorgio Maggiore, Santa Maria della Salute, and other churches.

How much time to allow

Allow 30 minutes to an hour to absorb the amazing interiors, and an extra 30 minutes if you decide to go up to the top of the bell tower.

16mm, f/11, ISO 100, 1/125 sec
CF 1.5x camera

3.02 Looking out at Basilica di San Giorgio Maggiore from Ponte dei Sospiri (Bridge of Sighs).

35mm, f/11, ISO 100, 1/250 sec
CF 1.5x camera

3.03 Basilica di San Giorgio Maggiore from the second storey balconies of Piazza San Marco.

Best time to visit

Despite its proximity to Piazza San Marco, Basilica di San Giorgio Maggiore is surprisingly quiet. Whilst you're in the neighbourhood, you can check out the nearby Cini Foundation arts centre, as well as the Teatro Verde open-air theatre.

55mm, f/5.6, ISO 125, 1/500 sec
FF camera

3.04 The arches of the cloisters of Basilica di San Giorgio Maggiore.

Tip

Access to Isola di San Giorgio Maggiore is by *vaporetto* only. When you disembark from the ferry, take a look at the timetable for upcoming options for your return trip (or moving on to the next island) to avoid, having to spend 20 minutes (or more) waiting for the next *vaporetto*.

Photo tips and tricks

Vantage points

Campanile di San Marco - For the best elevated view of Isola di San Giorgio Maggiore (including the Chiesa) and its position in the Venetian lagoon, look no further. Sunset is often the best time of day to capture the action.

Palazzo Ducale - You are spoilt for choice with views out over the lagoon. Best options are from the balconies.

Punta della Dogana - Standing on the tip of Dorsoduro out the front of Punta della Dogana provides a straight-on view of the basilica. Best views are in the evening to watch the sunset.

Piazza San Marco - Perhaps the easiest option listed here, you can include items of foreground interest in your photos (e.g. gondolas) in your compositions of the basilica.

Trinita water taxi pier - This is somewhat of a secret spot! If you follow the narrow lanes down to the water taxi pier, you'll get distance views of the basilica along with Punta della Dogana in the medium ground. Note that the wooden pier isn't the most stable surface for mounting a tripod, so you'll need to bump up your shutter speed.

105mm, f/5.6, ISO 1600, 1/125 sec
FF camera
3.06 Ornamental staff catching the afternoon sun streaming into the basilica.

11mm, f/11, ISO 100, 1.6 sec
CF 1.5x camera
3.05 Large Tintoretto paintings either side of the presbytery of the basilica.

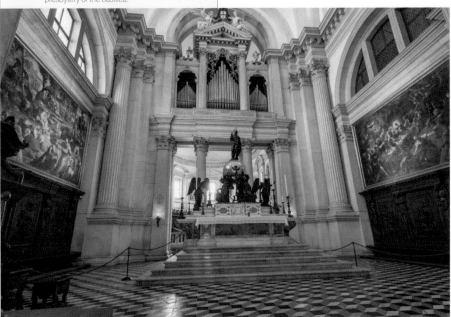

105mm, f/8, ISO 100, 1/800 sec
FF camera

3.07 Detailed statues and coat of arms on the exterior of the basilica.

12mm, f/11, ISO 50, 25 sec
CF 1.5x camera

3.08 Wooden details of the choir.

View from the top

Consider climbing the bell tower to get an elevated view of the lagoon, including towards Piazza San Marco. Note that this isn't the greatest location for sunrise or sunset photos due to opening hours.

3.09 | 24mm, f/11, ISO 400, 4 sec
FF camera
Sunrise looking over the basilica from the wooden Trinita water taxi pier.

Basilica di Santa Maria della Salute

This Baroque-style basilica was built at the end of the 18th century by Baldassare Longhena in honour of Saint Mary, and to celebrate survival of recent plagues. It is made from Istrian stone and the dome consists of a nave, three chapels, and coloured marble with flower decoration. Like all the other basilicas and churches in Venice, the interior of the Santa Maria della Salute contains the paintings of masters. The most prominent of these Titian's the "Marriage at Cana".

🌐 basilicasalutevenezia.it/

#basilicadisantamariadellasalute, #basilicadisantamaria

Tickets and opening times

🕐 Opening hours: 09:00 - 12:00 and 15:00 - 17:00 daily. Sunday services may change from time to time.

$ *Free*

Logistics

Photo tips and tricks

Vantage points

Campanile di San Marco - Elevated views of the Basilica nestled in with Punta della Dogana and the rest of Dorsoduro island.

Location information

🧭 Campo della Salute, Dorsoduro

⚓ Salute

 150mm, f/11, ISO 50, 1/6 sec
CF 1.5x camera
3.10 The domes of the basilica with a bright orange sunrise.

Trinita water taxi pier - This is somewhat of a secret spot! If you follow the narrow lanes down to the water taxi pier, you will be treated with a fronton view of the Basilica.

Note that the wooden pier isn't the most stable surface for mounting a tripod, so you'll need to bump up your shutter speed.

 75mm, f/7.1, ISO 1600, 1/60 sec
FF camera
3.12 You'll likely have the basilica to yourself so that you can capture the elaborate ornamentation.

 70mm, f/11, ISO 50, 1/15 sec
CF 1.5x camera
3.11 The sunrise view of the basilica along the Grand Canal is one of the iconic views of Venice.

135mm, f/10, ISO 100, 1/250 sec
CF 1.5x camera
3.13 Looking across at Chiesa di Santissimo Redentore from Punta della Dogana.

Chiesa di Santissimo Redentore (Il Redentore)

The church was built as a thanksgiving to Christ the Redeemer after a deadly plague hit the city. For almost five centuries, Venetians commemorate this event every third Sunday of July. Palladio built the Renaissance-style church on Giudecca in the 16th century with prominent features that include two bell towers on the sides of the cupola and lights that illuminate the interiors.

Logistics

Location information

 Campo del SS. Redentore, Giudecca

⚓ Redentore

🌐 en.turismovenezia.it/Venezia/Chiesadel-Redentore-Santissimo-Redentore-6069.html

\# #chiesadelsantissimoredentore

Tickets and opening times

🕐 Monday to Saturday: 10:00 - 17:00 (last entrance 16:45).
Sunday: *closed*

$ €3 / €1.50

200mm, f/5.6, ISO 400, 1/320 sec
CF 1.5x camera
3.14 Sunset view from the south side of Dorsoduro.

200mm, f/5.6, ISO 400, 1/320 sec
CF 1.5x camera

3.15   Sunset view from the Campanile di San Marco.

28mm, f/8, ISO 100, 1/320 sec
FF camera

3.16   Front-on view from the *vaporetto*.

▎Photo tips and tricks

Owing to its prominent position, it's possible to capture the Chiesa from different angles along the South side of Dorsoduro island.

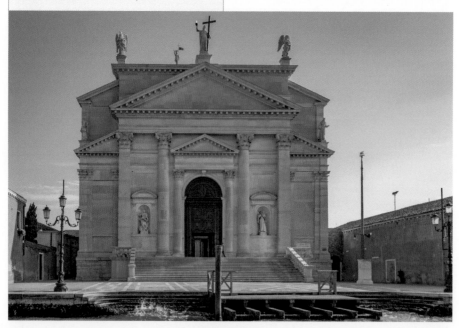

Chiesa di Francesco della Vigna

Constructed on the site of a vineyard (Vigna) by Franciscan monks, this is the site where an angel is supposed to have appeared to Saint Mark and pronounced the city's motto "*Pax tibi Evangelista meus*" (Peace be unto you, Mark my Evangelist). The Franciscans first constructed the church in 1253 CE to honour

Saint Francis of Assisi, considered a man of dialogue. In 1534, Doge Andrea Gritti wanted to revitalise the area, so he sponsored the reconstruction of a church designed and built by Jacopino Sansovino. The *campanile* (bell tower) is modelled after the original in Piazza San Marco, without many of the added flourishes.

11mm, f/11, ISO 100, 1/125 sec
CF 1.5x camera
3.20 The empty cloiser next to the *chiesa*.

There are several classic art pieces inside, so take your time.

Logistics

Logistics

⊘ Campo San Francesco, Castello

⚓ Celestia

🌐 en.turismovenezia.it/Venezia/Chiesadi-San-Francesco-della-Vigna-6099.html

#chiesadisanfrancescodellavigna

Tickets and opening times

🕐 08:00 - 12:30 and 15:00 – 19:00 daily.

$ *Free*

200mm, f/11, ISO 800, 1/160 sec
CF 1.5x camera
3.21 View of the Chiesa della Madonna dell'Orto around sunset from Campanile di San Marco.

CHURCHES

Map 3.2: Chiesa di Francesco della Vigna.

24mm, f/8, ISO 100, 1/160 sec
FF camera
3.22
The restored cloister of the chiesa with art display under the arches.

Chiesa della Madonna dell'Orto

Originally constructed to venerate Saint Christopher (Patron saint of travellers), its name came from a legend of a statue of the Madonna rescued from a nearby orchard (orto) and placed here. Standing on the northernmost edge of the Sestiere of Cannaregio, this majestic and imposing Gothic church still has the original paving brick laid out in a herring-bone pattern. Originally built in the 14th century, it required reconstruction in the 15th century.

🌐 en.turismovenezia.it/Venezia/Chiesa-della-Madonna-dell-Orto-6072.html

\# #madonnadellorto

Tickets and opening times

🕐 Monday to Saturday: 10:00 - 17:00.
Sunday: *closed*

$ €3 / €1.50

▌ Logistics

▌ Photo tips and tricks

Spend a little time in the shade of the cloister which has magnificent views of the church. You can see and admire many of Tintoretto's works inside.

Location information

⊘ Fondamenta Madonna dell'Orto, Cannaregio

⚓ S. Giorgio

28mm, f/5.6, ISO 100, 1/640 sec
FF camera
3.23   Portrait photos are ideal for church facades.

30mm, f/11, ISO 100, 4 sec
FF camera
3.25   Using the pews as a surface for long-exposures.

24mm, f/11, ISO 100, 3.2 sec
FF camera
3.24   Long-exposure shot taken from top of pews.

24mm, f/5.6, ISO 1600, 1/25 sec
FF camera
3.26   The sumptuous interiors of I Frari.

Basilica di Santa Maria Gloriosa dei Frari (I Frari)

Considered one of the greatest churches in Venice, this minor basilica traces its origins as far back as 1250 CE when Franciscan monks were granted the lands. The current Italian Gothic style church was consecrated in 1492, although its *campanile* (bell tower) was completed by 1396 CE. The interior is sumptuous, even by Venetian standards, and contains Titian's iconic "Madonna of the Assumption". Fittingly, the master painter is interred here too.

Logistics

200mm, f/5.6, ISO 400, 1/320 sec
CF 1.5x camera
3.27   The large *campo* surrounding the basilica is great for people watching.

Location information

◎   Campo dei Frari, San Polo

⚓   S. Toma'

🌐   en.turismovenezia.it/Venezia/Basilicadi-Santa-Maria-Gloriosa-dei-Frari-6053.html

#basilicadeifrari, #ifrari

Tickets and opening times

🕐   Monday to Saturday: 09:00 - 18:00.
Sunday: 13:00 - 18:00.

$ €3 / €1.50

 16mm, f/8, ISO 800, 1/15 sec
CF 1.5x camera

3.28 People in frame help give a sense of scale - a way to use the crowds to your advantage!

 16mm, f/8, ISO 800, 1/15 sec
CF 1.5x camera

3.29 Take in the details of I Frari.

Chiesa di Santa Maria dei Miracoli

Covered by polychrome marbles, the church earns the nickname "Marble church". This jewel box is a classic example of Venetian Renaissance style with its single nave and extensive barrel vault. Inside the church are ornamental marble staircases and statues by Nicolo di Pietro, Tulio Lombardo, and Alessandro Vittoria. The interior roof contains 50 small scenes of prophets painted in detail.

Logistics

Location information

11mm, f/11, ISO 100, 1/200 sec
CF 1.5x camera

3.31   Wide-angle shot of "jewel box" design.

⊘   Campiello dei Miracoli, Cannaregio

⚓   Rialto or F. te. Nove.

🌐   en.turismovenezia.it/Venezia/Chiesadi-Santa-Maria-dei-Miracoli-6148.html

#santamariadeimiracoli

Tickets and opening times

🕐   Monday to Saturday: 10:00 - 17:00 (last entry 16:45).
Sunday: 10:00 - 17:30.

$ €3 / €1.50

Other important Venetian churches

3.32 28mm, f/9, ISO 100, 1/500 sec
CF 1.5x camera
Chiesa di San Barnaba, made famous by scenes from *Raiders of the Lost Ark*.

Basilica dei Santi Giovanni e Paolo (San Zanipolo)

The main Dominican church of Venice (known as San Zanipolo in Venetian), this minor basilica was actually dedicated to two obscure soldier-martyrs named John and Paul, not the saints. Built in the 1430s, the

3.33 11mm, f/11, ISO 100, 1/200 sec
CF 1.5x camera
Wide-angle shot of the basilica.

Italian Gothic church hosted the funerals of all of Venice's Doges from this time and 25 of them are buried on the grounds.

Logistics

🧭 Campo SS. Giovanni e Paolo, Castello

⚓ Ospedale

🌐 en.turismovenezia.it/Venezia/Basilica-of-Santi-Giovanni-e-Paolo-San-Zanipolo-6066.html

\# #santigiovanniepaolo

🕐 07:30 - 18:30 daily.

💲 €3.50 / €1.50

Photo tips and tricks

Unfortunately, no photos are allowed to be taken inside.

85mm, f/8, ISO 100, 1/160 sec
CF 1.5x camera

3.34 Sunset view of Basilica dei Santi Giovanni e Paolo from Campanile di San Marco.

Logistics

⊘ Campo San Pantalon, San Polo

⚓ S. Toma'

🌐 www.sanpantalon.it/

\# #sanpantalon

🕐 Monday to Saturday: 10:00 - 12:00 and 13:00 - 15:00.
Sunday: *closed*

$ *Free*

Chiesa di San Pantalon

This 17th century church dedicated to Saint Pantaleon isn't particularly impressive outside, however reserve judgement until you stick your head in! The astonishing ceiling fresco "The Martyrdom and Apotheosis of St Pantalon" by Fumiani has to be seen to be believed.

24mm, f/8, ISO 100, 1/400 sec
FF camera

3.35 The unassuming facade of Chiesa di S. Pantalon.

Photo tips and tricks

Unfortunately, no photos are allowed to be taken inside.

Chiesa di San Zaccaria

The resting place of St. Zacharias, father of John the Baptist, was mostly a monastery over the centuries. According to tradition, the abbess of the convent of San Zaccaria gave the first ducal horn, the precious headgear of the doge in 864 CE in return for an annual

3.36 24mm, f/8, ISO 100, 4 sec
FF camera
Using the pews to take a long-exposure shot of the interior of the *chiesa*.

visit. The original church was built in the 9th century to hold the body of San Zaccaria. The present church, however, was constructed between 1458 and 1515. This is one of the most decorated interior churches in Venice, complete with wall-to-wall works from 17th and 18th century artists.

3.37 24mm, f/8, ISO 100, 3.2 sec
FF camera
The body of San Zaccaria inside the *chiesa*.

Logistics

⊘ Campo S. Zaccaria, Castello

⚓ S Zaccaria

🌐 en.turismovenezia.it/Venezia/Chiesadi-San-Zaccaria-6139.html

#sanzaccaria

🕐 Monday to Saturday: 10:00 - 12:00 and 16:00 - 18:00.
Sunday: 16:00 - 18:00

$ *Free*

Chiesa di San Giacomo dell Orio

Founded around the 9th century, the church is dedicated to St James the Apostle, and is known for its ship's keel roof.

Logistics

⊘ Campo San Giaccomo dall'Orio, Santa Croce

⚓ San Stae or Riva de Biasio

11mm, f/11, ISO 100, 1/200 sec
CF 1.5x camera

3.38 Ship's keel roof design of the interior of Chiesa di
San Giacomo dell'Orio.

🌐 en.turismovenezia.it/Venezia/Chiesadi-San-Giacomo-dall-Orio-6.16.html

\# #sangiacomodallorio, #sangiacomodellorio

🕐 Monday to Saturday: 10:00 - 17:00.
Sunday: *closed*

$ €3 / €1.50

▌ Chiesa dell'Angelo Raffaele

An out-of-the-way church harking back as early as 416 CE, the church is dedicated

11mm, f/11, ISO 100, 1/200 sec
CF 1.5x camera

3.39 Exterior of Chiesa dell'Angelo Raffaele.

to the Archangel Raphael (Patron saint of fishermen). The original structure was destroyed by three fires that happened in 899, 1106, and 1149 CE. No records existed when the church was built, but according to traditions, it was built in the 7th century under Saint Magnus, who had been the bishop of Oderzo at that time.

Logistics

📍 Campo dell'Anzolo Rafael, Dorsoduro

⚓ S. Basillio

🌐 en.turismovenezia.it/Venezia/AngeloRaffaele-6046.html

\# #anzolorafael

🕐 Monday to Saturday: 10:00 - 12:00 and 15:00 - 17:30.
Sunday: 09:00 - 12:00.

$ *Free*

Chiesa di San Giacomo di Rialto (San Giacometto)

50mm, f/5.6, ISO 100, 1/80 sec
FF camera

3.40   Clockface of Chiesa di San Giacomo di Rialto.

Said to be the oldest church in Venice, it is notable now for being almost entirely swallowed up by the nearby Rialto market. This church features a beautiful sundial and Gothic portico, and a clock that never tells the correct time! The connection between the church and the market is evident through a Latin inscription that encourages merchants to operate with honesty and fairness.

Logistics

⊘ Campo San Giacomo di Rialto, San Polo

⚓ Rialto or Rialto Mercato

🌐 en.turismovenezia.it/Venezia/SanGiacometto-Giacomo-di-Rialto-6186.html

\# #sangiacomodirialto

🕐 Monday to Saturday: 10:00 - 17:00.
Sunday: *closed*

$ *Free*

Chiesa di San Moise

The elaborate 17th century Baroque façade is the fascinating entrance to a church dedicated to Moses. The original building was built in the 10th century, with a Venetian-style bell tower dating from the 14th century.

Logistics

⊘ Campo San Moisè, San Marco

⚓ S. Marco

🌐 en.turismovenezia.it/Venezia/Chiesadi-San-Moisé-6.18.html

\# #sanmoise

🕐 15:30 - 19:00 daily, although the church is often open in the mornings as well.

$ *Free*

3.41 | 24mm, f/11, ISO 200, 1/80 sec
FF camera
The facade of Chiesa di San Moise.

Logistics

⊘ Campo dei Frari, San Polo

⚓ S. Toma'

🌐 www.scuolagrandesanrocco.org/home-en/

\# #chiesadisanrocco

🕐 08:00 - 12:30 to 15:00 - 17:00 daily.

$ *Free*

Chiesa di San Rocco

This place of worship is dedicated to San Rocco, the patron saint of plague victims. Built by Bartolomeo Bon between 1489 and 1508, the Church of San Rocco has a single nave with an apse presbytery and two chapels on the sides. It is also one of the churches built during that time to ward off the plague that killed many people in Venice. Several works by Tintoretto can be seen inside.

Chiesa di San Barnaba

Neoclassical church dedicated to the Apostle Barnabas with an impressive 13th century *campanile* (bell tower). In 1810, Napoleon issued a decree to close the church for worship. It is now used to host "temporary" exhibitions (the current Leonardo da Vinci machines exhibit has been open for years now).

3.42 | 11mm, f/11, ISO 50, 15 sec
CF 1.5x camera
Long-exposure day shot of Chiesa di San Rocco.

Logistics

⊘ Campo San Barnaba, Dorsoduro

⚓ Ca' Rezzonico

🌐 en.turismovenezia.it/Venezia/Chiesadi-San-Barnaba-6093.html

\# #chiesadisanbarnaba

🕐 The church is currently closed as a place of worship.

🕐 15:30 - 19:00 daily, although the church is often open in the mornings as well.

$ *Free*

Chiesa di Santa Maria del Giglio (Santa Maria Zobenigo)

Similar in style to Chiesa di San Moise, this church is somewhat tucked away for those seeking some quiet. Its façade was the work of Giuseppe Sardi while its interiors are adorned by the works of Antonio Zanchi, Gianbattista Crosato, Jacopo Marieschi, and Gaspare Diziani.

Logistics

⊘ Campo Santa Maria del Giglio, San Marco

⚓ S. Maria del Giglio

🌐 en.turismovenezia.it/Venezia/Chiesadi-Santa-Maria-del-Giglio-Zobenigo-6149.html

\# #santamariazobenigo

🕐 Monday to Saturday: 10:00 - 17:00 (last entry 16:45).
Sunday: 10:00 - 17:30.

$ €3 / €1.50

▌Chiesa di San Sebastiano

This somewhat out of the way church was dedicated to Saint Sebastian for delivering Venice from the plague in 1468 CE. Numerous works of art inside include many by Veronese (who was interred here), as well as works by Tintoretto and Titian.

Logistics

⊘ Campo San Sebastiano, Dorsoduro

⚓ S. Basilio

🌐 en.turismovenezia.it/Venezia/Chiesa-di-San-Sebastiano-6136.html

\# #chiesadisansebastiano

28mm, f/11, ISO 250, 1/500 sec
FF camera
3.43 The quiet area around Chiesa di San Sebastiano.

30mm, f/8, ISO 100, 1/250 sec
FF camera
3.44 The facade of Chiesa di Santa Maria del Giglio.

35mm, f/11, ISO 160, 1/250 sec
FF camera

3.45 Chiesa di San Simeone Piccolo at sunset.

Chiesa di San Simeone Piccolo

A relative newcomer by Venice standards (built in 1738 CE), the church is named after Saints Simeon and Jude. It is commonly referred to as San Simeon Piccolo to distinguish it from the nearby church of San Simeone Profeta (San Simeon Grande). The bold Neoclassical design greets those who arrive in Venice by train. It has a unique circular shape, which is the first church in Venice to have this feature. But what distinguishes this church from others is the remarkable octagonal cemetery crypt, the only catacomb complex in Venice.

Logistics

⊘ Fondamenta San Simeone Piccolo, Santa Croce

⚓ Ca' Rezzonico

🌐 en.turismovenezia.it/Venezia/San-Simeone-Piccolo-o-San-Simeone-eGiuda-6193.html

\# #sansimeonepiccolo

🕐 The church is currently closed.

Chiesa di Santa Maria del Rosario

The building was built under the religious order of the Dominicans who lived in the convent and the church of Santa Maria della Visitazione. The project was led by Giorgio Massari (1686 - 1766), and was modelled (both inside and out) on Il Redentore to its South East.

Logistics

⊘ Fondamenta delle Zattere ai Gesuati, Dorsoduro

⚓ Zattere

🌐 en.turismovenezia.it/Venezia/Chiesa-di-Santa-Maria-del-Rosario-Chiesa-deiGesuati-6150.html

#santamariadelrosario

🕐 Monday to Saturday: 10:00 - 17:00 (last entry 16:45).
Sunday: 14:00 - 17:30.

$ €3 / €1.50

 105mm, f/11, ISO 160, 1/250 sec
FF camera
3.46 Chiesa di Santa Maria del Rosario from the canal.

Chiesa di Santa Maria Formosa

The tradition of the name of this 1504 CE church is that the Virgin Mary appeared to the then Bishop of Oderzo St Magnus in the form of a voluptuous woman (*formosa* in Italian).

 105mm, f/6.3, ISO 250, 1/125 sec
CF 1.5x camera
3.47 Interesting statues and ornamentation above the entrance to Chiesa di Santa Maria Formosa.

24mm, f/11, ISO 250, 1/80 sec
FF camera

3.48 Chiesa di Santo Stefano at sunset.

The Tribuno family contributed financially to the construction of the church dedicated to the Purification of the Blessed Virgin, which was later renamed Santa Maria Formosa.

The interior has to be seen to be believed, including its ship's keel roof and marble. The church was built in the 13th century by the friars of Sant'Agostino dedicated to the first martyrs of Christianity.

Logistics

- ◎ Campo Santa Maria Formosa, Castello

- ⚓ Ospedale

- ⊕ en.turismovenezia.it/Venezia/Chiesadi-Santa-Maria-Formosa-6155.html

- # #santamariaformosa

- ◷ Monday to Saturday: 10:00 - 17:00. Sunday: *closed*

- $ €3 / €1.50

Logistics

- ◎ Campo Santo Stefano, San Marco

- ⚓ S. Angelo, S. Samuele, and S. Maria del Giglio

- ⊕ en.turismovenezia.it/Venezia/Chiesadi-Santo-Stefano-Protomartire-6161.html

- # #chiesasantostefano

- ◷ Monday to Saturday: 10:00 - 17:00 (last entry 16:45). Sunday: 12:00 - 17:30.

- $ *Free*

▌Chiesa di Santo Stefano

This large Gothic parish church occupies the North end of Campo Santo Stefano.

Basilica di San Pietro di Castello

The official church of Venice from 1451 up to 1807 CE, despite it being somewhat out of the way. It hasn't fared so well since then, with the leaning *campanile* (bell tower) bearing testament to this.

Monday to Saturday: 10:00 - 17:00.
Sunday: *closed*

€3 / €1.50

Logistics

⊘ Sestiere Castello

⚓ S. Pietro di Castello

🌐 en.turismovenezia.it/Venezia/Basilica-Concattedrale-di-San-Pietro-di-Castello-6049.html

\# #sanpietrodicastello

80mm, f/11, ISO 250, 1/250 sec
FF camera
3.50 The campanile of Basilica di S Pietro di Castello.

105mm, f/7.1, ISO 400, 1/125 sec
FF camera
3.49 Cloister of Basilica di San Pietro di Castello.

11mm, f/11, ISO 100, 1/60 sec
CF 1.5x camera
3.51 The facade of Chiesa di S Giacomo dell'Orio.

4.00 | 70mm, f/11, ISO 50, 1/3 sec FF camera | Sunset over Punta della Dogana and the Venetian lagoon from Campanile di San Marco.

Palaces, museums, and landmarks

There is more to Venice than Piazza San Marco (St Mark's Square), the Rialto bridge and gondolas! The Venetian Republic was one of the largest financial and maritime powers in Europe during the Middle Ages and up to the 17th century. Known as a financier and patron of the arts and architectural styles, Venice still has numerous venues and museums dedicated to celebrating its former glory. For those in search of an art fix, a break from taking photos, or to escape the rain or cold, Venice has more museums and galleries than you could poke a gondola oar at. Consider these venues as places to visit to understand more about life in Venice over the centuries.

 50mm, f/4, ISO 1000, 1/50 sec FF camera

4.01 "*Rialto no se toca*", roughly "Don't mess with Rialto" - locals wanting to retain their traditions.

Rialto mercato
(Rialto market)

The Rialto market is one of the most important and ancient markets in Italy and is one of the obligatory stops for those visiting the city of Venice. The main fish and fresh grocery market of Venice, it has been a hub of commercial activity since the 11th century. Located near the Rialto Bridge, it stretches between Campo San Giacomo di Rialto and Campo della Pescaria and hosts the famous fish market and the fruit and vegetable market. The *Merceria* path would lead mariners and traders from Piazza San Marco to here to ply their wares. The market is divided into a fruit and vegetable market (Erbaria) and a picturesque fish market (Pescaria). You have to pay a visit to the

market to enjoy the true flavours of Venetian food and wine products that are harvested from the surrounding areas.

24mm, f/8, ISO 800, 1/60 sec
FF camera
4.02 The interior of the *mercato* is quite dark, so use high ISO, wide angles, or fast shutter speeds.

28mm, f/8, ISO 200, 1/60 sec
FF camera
4.03 Fish for sale in the *mercato*.

Logistics

- ⊘ Campo della Pescaria, San Polo
- ⚓ Rialto Mercato
- \# #rialtomercato, #rialtomarket

This is a functioning market so please be respectful of the sellers and patrons.

Tickets and opening times

- 🕐 07:00 - 14:00 daily. Much of the fresh seafood is gone by 09:00 each morning.
- \$ *Free*

How much time to allow

Allow 30 minutes to an hour to explore the markets and perhaps try some of the wares.

50mm, f/8, ISO 1600, 1/60 sec
FF camera

4.04   Fresh produce - what the locals will eat tonight.

Photo tips and tricks

Low-light

The majority of the market is inside dim concrete structures or under tarpaulins. Consider cranking up your ISO and open your aperture as much as possible. Large aperture prime lenses are a great idea here, such as a "nifty fifty" 50mm f/1.4 or f/1.8.

50mm, f/8, ISO 500, 1/100 sec
FF camera

4.05   Bringing in the morning's catch for the market.

 16mm, f/8, ISO 400, 1/20 sec
CF 1.5x camera

4.06   Main entrance to the fish market of the *mercato*.

 35mm, f/6.3, ISO 400, 1/60 sec
CF 1.5x camera

4.07   See the seafood that Venetians eat day-to-day.

Punta della Dogana

Originally a customs house built in the 17th century, Punta della Dogana sits at the entrance of the Grand Canal and served to collect taxes from inbound ships entering the city. The building was converted in 2009 into an art exhibition space.

70mm, f/13, ISO 100, 1/250 sec
CF 1.5x camera
4.09 Weathervane on top of Punta della Dogana.

Logistics

Location information

⊘ Fondamenta Salute, Dorsoduro

⚓ Salute

🌐 www.palazzograssi.it/en/about/sites/punta-della-dogana/

◎ @palazzo_grassi

\# #puntadelladogana, #puntadelladoganamuseum

Tickets and opening times

🕐 Wednesday to Monday: 10:00 - 17:00 (last entry is 18:00).
Tuesday: *closed*

$ €18 / €15 (Palazzo Grassi and Punta della Dogana)

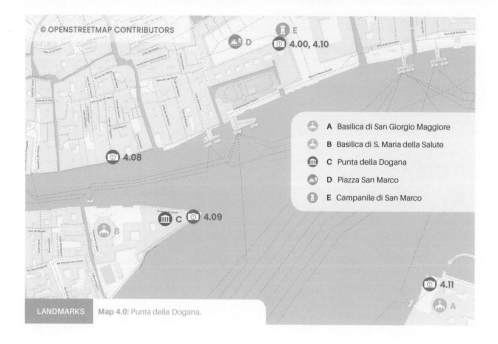

© OPENSTREETMAP CONTRIBUTORS

D
E
4.00, 4.10

4.08

A Basilica di San Giorgio Maggiore
B Basilica di S. Maria della Salute
C Punta della Dogana
D Piazza San Marco
E Campanile di San Marco

C 4.09

B

4.11

A

LANDMARKS **Map 4.0:** Punta della Dogana.

60mm, f/11, ISO 50, 3.2 sec
FF camera

4.10 Blue hour over Punta della Dogana and the
Venetian lagoon from Campanile di San Marco.

Photo tips and tricks

Vantage points

Campanile di San Marco - The best elevated view of Punta della Dogana and its position at the entrance to the Grand Canal. Aim to be there for dramatic sunsets.

Giudecca - Owing to its key position on Dorsoduro island, it's possible to capture pictures of Punta della Dogana from along the north side of Giudecca.

Basilica di San Giorgio Maggiore - Stand outside of the church, just as you exit the *vaporetto* service, and face Punta della Dogana. This affords an almost front-on view facing West. Best views are in the morning (with the Eastern sun) using a telephoto lens.

Trinita water taxi pier - This is somewhat of a secret spot! If you follow the narrow lanes down to the water taxi pier, you'll be treated with a medium distance view of Punta della Dogana. Note that the wooden pier isn't the most stable surface for mounting a tripod, so you'll need to bump up your shutter speed.

Weathervane

The weathervane on top of Punta della Dogana is known as Fortuna. This statue is mounted on top of a large golden ball held up by two slaves. As the weather vane rotates in the wind, a long-exposure shot can help add this drama to the photo. This will require a Neutral Density filter during the day.

90mm, f/11, ISO 100, 1/250 sec
FF camera

4.11   View from Isola di San Giorgio Maggiore.

4.12 75mm, f/11, ISO 125, 1/250 sec
FF camera
Late afternoon sun over the main entrance to the
Arsenale di Venezia.

Arsenale di Venezia

The place where the Venetian Republic built and repaired its naval prowess, first built in 1104 CE. This was the largest industrial area in Europe before the Industrial Revolution. Employing up to 16,000 workers in its heyday, it was rumoured to be able to produce an entire ship, fully fitted, in a day!

Logistics

Location information

⌖ Arsenale di Venezia, Castello

⚓ Arsenale

🌐 www.comune.venezia.it/it/
arsenaledivenezia (in Italian)

\# #arsenaledivenezia

Tickets and opening times

The arsenal is still an active naval base, so you are limited to where you can access. Some parts of the arsenal are open as part of the Biennale celebrations for art exhibitions.

Photo tips and tricks

Vantage points

Main "entrance" view - If there are not many people around, you can use a telephoto zoom lens to capture the main entrance from points along Fondamenta Arsenale (facing North).

Appreciating the scale - The walls of the Arsenale are quite extensive (to keep out prying eyes) however walking around the

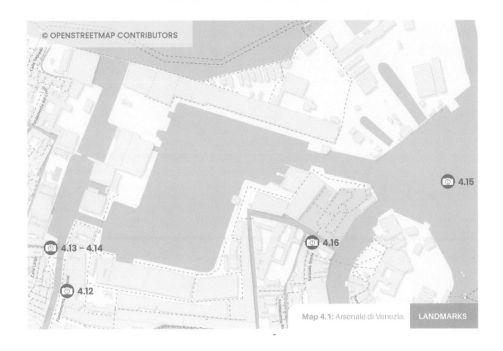

 4.12

 4.13 – 4.14

4.16

4.15

Map 4.1: Arsenale di Venezia. LANDMARKS

4.13 45mm, f/8, ISO 100, 1/400 sec
FF camera
Statue of Neptune at the Arsenal main entrance.

4.14 105mm, f/8, ISO 100, 1/400 sec
FF camera
Ornate clock at the Arsenal main entrance.

105mm, f/8, ISO 125, 1/400 sec
FF camera

4.15 The main marine entrance of the Arsenal (from a boat).

neighbouring streets and canals will give a sense of size of the shipyards.

100mm, f/8, ISO 100, 1/320 sec
FF camera

4.16 The expansive walls of the Arsenale.

28mm, f/11, ISO 250, 1/200 sec
FF camera

4.17   The heart of the Jewish quarter of Venice.

Ghetto Nuovo
(Jewish quarter)

Originally a foundry area (ghetto), this island was gated up to create the Jewish quarter from 1516 CE until Napoleon's overthrowing of the Venetian Republic. Allowed out during the day, Jewish people were locked away each evening and on holidays. Despite this, Jewish communities from around Europe continued to move here, and so had to build upwards to accommodate the additional people. This can be seen by the fact that the synagogues that were built here were quite ethnically distinct: Italian (Scuola Italiana), Spanish (Scuola Spagnola), German (Scuola Grande Tedesca), Levantine Sephardi community (Scola Levantina), and the Scuola Canton for the Ashkenazic Jews.

Although they were finally recognised as Venetian citizens under Napoleon, the local Jewish population was decimated by Mussolini's Fascist government. Sadly, most of the thousands that lived here met their fate in concentration camps during World War II. Today there are around 450 Jewish people living in Venice, spread out across the city.

105mm, f/5.6, ISO 100, 1/400 sec
FF camera

4.18   Entrance to a kosher garden restaurant.

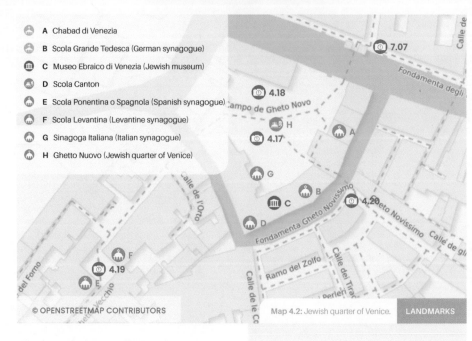

A Chabad di Venezia

B Scola Grande Tedesca (German synagogue)

C Museo Ebraico di Venezia (Jewish museum)

D Scola Canton

E Scola Ponentina o Spagnola (Spanish synagogue)

F Scola Levantina (Levantine synagogue)

G Sinagoga Italiana (Italian synagogue)

H Ghetto Nuovo (Jewish quarter of Venice)

© OPENSTREETMAP CONTRIBUTORS

Map 4.2: Jewish quarter of Venice.   LANDMARKS

Check out the Museo Ebraico di Venezia (Jewish Museum of Venice) to learn about the history of the Jewish citizens of Venice.

Logistics

Location information

⊘ Campo di Ghetto Nuovo, Cannaregio

⚓ Guglie

🌐 www.museoebraico.it/en/

📷 @museoebraicove

\# #museoebraico, #ghettonuovo

Museum tickets and opening times

🕐 1st June to 30th September - 10:00 to 19:00.
1st October to 31st May - 10:00 to 17:30.
Saturdays: *closed*

$ €8 / €6

$ €8 / €6

www.coopculture.it/en/ticket.
cfm?office=Museo%20Ebraico%20di%20Venezia&id=38

Museum entrance + tour of three synagogues

$ €12 / €10

www.coopculture.it/en/ticket.
cfm?office=Museo%20Ebraico%20di%20Venezia&id=38

Luggage / bags

Note: there is security for the museum and larger bags can't be taken inside.

Photo tips and tricks

Photography inside the synagogues is not permitted during the tours.

35mm, f/8, ISO 125, 1/320 sec
FF camera
4.19 Entrance to the Levantine synagogue.

30mm, f/11, ISO 125, 1/125 sec
FF camera
4.20 The South East entrance to the Jewish quarter.

 4.21　14mm, f/8, ISO 125, 1/250 sec
FF camera
Ultra-wide lens required to capture everything.

Scala Contarini
del Bovolo

A staircase more famous than the building it was constructed for, the six-storey spiral marvel catches the first-time visitor by surprise. Built in 1499 when external staircases were more common, this Renaissance period gem is a must-see for those with a passion for Venetian architecture.

Logistics

Location information

⊘ Palazzo Contarini del Bovolo, San Marco

⚓ Rialto

🌐 www.gioiellinascostidivenezia.it/en/the-jewels/scala-contarini-del-bovolo/

\# #scalacontarinidelbovolo, #contarinidelbovolo

Tickets and opening times

🕐 10:00 - 18:00 daily (last entry is 17:30).

💲 €7 / €6

Photo tips and tricks

The spiral staircase is in the courtyard of Palazzo Contarini del Bovolo, and the entry fee includes access to the staircase. You can enter the courtyard during the day and take photos of the staircase through the fence at night.

4.22 14mm, f/8, ISO 200, 5 sec
FF camera
Ultra-wide view of Teatro la Fenice.

Teatro la Fenice

The Phoenix ("La Fenice") theatre seems to have been prophetically named as it has burned down three times since 1774, and so named in reference to the company's ability to rise from the ashes like a Phoenix. Famous across Europe, many composers have premiered operas here including Verdi's La Traviata, as works by Bellini, Donizetti, and Rossini.

Logistics

Location information

⊘ Campo San Fantin, San Marco

⚓ S. Maria del Giglio

🌐 www.teatrolafenice.it/en/

📷 @teatrolafenice

\# #teatrolafenice, #teatrolafenicevenezia

Tickets and opening times

🕐 10:00 - 17:00 daily.

$ €11 / €7 (self-guided tour).

4.23 105mm, f/11, ISO 100, 3.2 sec
FF camera
The ornate (and private) theatre boxes.

There is a self-guided tour audio guide available in several languages at the entrance (the audio guide is free, and essential). If you are lucky, you could be inside during stage setup or orchestra rehearsal. If you are interested in seeing a show, ensure that you book tickets well in advance. Prices can give Broadway and the West End a run for their money.

Photo tips and tricks

Patience

A little patience pays off, as you may need to wait for small crowds to pass through before you can get the photo that you're after.

Upper balconies

The upper balconies, part of the tour route, provide an excellent place to capture the splendour of the theatre. Don't forget to check out the ceiling!

 105mm, f/5.6, ISO 400, 1/200 sec
FF camera

4.25   The phoenix watching over Teatro la Fenice.

 24mm, f/11, ISO 400, 2.5 sec
FF camera

4.24   Use the gap between seats to hold the camera.

24mm, f/5.6, ISO 1600, 1/25 sec
FF camera
4.26   Tubs (and boats) keep books off the ground.

Libreria Acqua Alta

A modern curiosity compared with the majority of places featured in this guide, this bookstore is definitely built to live with the *acqua alta* (high water) that can afflict the city. Check out the gondola bookshelf, the numerous bathtubs and crates used to keep books elevated, the cute courtyard, the entry point to the nearby canal (at the back of the shop) and the rear courtyard with "stairs" to view the nearby canal.

Tickets and opening times

🕒   09:00 - 20:00 daily.

$ *Free*

▌Logistics

Location information

⊘   Calle Lunga Santa Maria Formosa, Castello

⚓   Ospedale

◎   @libreriaacquaalta

\#   #libreriaacquaalta, #libreriaacquaaltavenezia

24mm, f/5.6, ISO 1600, 1/30 sec
FF camera
4.27   Gondola-shaped bookshelf in the store.

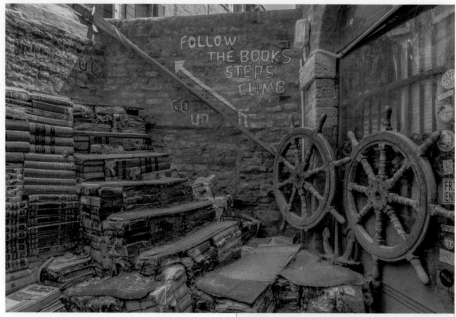

This is a bookstore and so has paying customers during the day. Please be courteous to others, including wearing your backpack on your front so that you don't knock others (or books).

	24mm, f/11, ISO 400, 1/40 sec
	FF camera
4.28	Rear courtyard with book staircase to the canal.

	24mm, f/11, ISO 1000, 1/30 sec
	FF camera
4.29	The small courtyard surrounded by old books.

100mm, f/5.6, ISO 1600, 1/50 sec
FF camera
4.30
The winged lion of St Mark holding a bible on the prow of a ship at Museo Storico Navale.

Museums
and galleries

If you are a history buff, Venice has one of the most important museum systems in the world. The indoor venues are great for escaping the heat (and crowds) of the middle of the day and are a perfect solution to a rainy day.

Some museums and galleries don't allow photography inside, and this is clearly marked at the entrances. It is invariably dark inside the majority of museums and galleries, particularly from your camera's perspective. A high ISO and / or wider apertures can best help capture the impressive details inside.

Museo Storico Navale

Established by the Italian Navy in 1919, the museum occupies a former factory for gondola oars. Exhibits in the 42 rooms includes much of the maritime traditions that Venice was famous for over the centuries, and also includes more modern fare from World War I and II.

Location information

⊘ Riva San Biagio, Castello

⚓ Arsenale

🌐 www.visitmuve.it/en/museums/naval-historical-museum/

#museostoriconavale

24mm, f/6.3, ISO 800, 1/25 sec
FF camera

4.31 Royal Barge for Victor Emmanuel II in 1866.

Tickets and opening times

Venice Naval History Museum
🕐 1st April to 31st October - 10:00 to 18:00 (last entry at 17:00).
1st November to 31st March - 10:00 to 17:00 (last entry is 16:00).

Ships pavilion
🕐 1st April to 31st October - 11:00 to 18:00 (last entry at 17:00).
1st November to 31st March - 11:00 to 17:00 (last entry is 16:00).

💲 €10 / €7.50

Ca' d'Oro

This "House of Gold", named after the gold leaf decorative features on the windows, is one of the most photographed buildings along the Grand Canal. Modelled after the Palazzo Ducale in Gothic style, this state-owned treasure now functions as a gallery. Formerly a patrician palace that dates back to the 15th century, the Ca' d'Oro is now a museum that houses the art collection of Baron Giorgio Franchetti.

Location information

⊘ Fondamenta Trapolin, Cannaregio

⚓ Ca' d'Oro

🌐 www.cadoro.org/?lang=en

📷 @galleriagiorgiofranchetti

\# #cadoro, #cadorovenezia

Tickets and opening times

🕐 Tuesday to Sunday: 08:15 to 19:15. Monday: 08:15 to 14:00.

💲 €8.50 / €2

 70mm, f/8, ISO 100, 1/125 sec
FF camera
4.32 The iconic facade of Ca d'Oro.

Ca' Pesaro

Named after the patron family that owned the building, this palace was designed by architect Longheni, also responsible for Ca' Rezzonico and Chiesa di Santa Maria della Salute. It is now a modern art museum of 19th and 20th century Italian art.

Location information

⊘ Fondamenta de Ca' Pesaro, Santa Croce

⚓ San Stae

🌐 capesaro.visitmuve.it/en/home/

📷 @museocapesaro

\# #capesaro, #capesaromuseumofmodernart

Tickets and opening times

🕐 Tuesday to Sunday: 10:30 to 18:00.
Monday: *closed*

💲 €10 / €7.50

Ca' Rezzonico

Magnificent rooms with valuable frescoes, exceptional furniture, tapestries on the walls, Murano glass chandeliers - these are just some of the things you will find in this museum. But the most surprising element is certainly the presence of a pharmacy: a real spice shop with majolica pots, a laboratory, and all the original equipment necessary for the preparation of medicines.

Location information

⊘ Fondamenta Rezzonico, Dorsoduro

⚓ Ca' Rezzonico

🌐 carezzonico.visitmuve.it/en/home/

\# #carezzonico

Tickets and opening times

🕐 1st April to 31st October - 10:30 to 18:00.
1st November to 31st March - 10:30
to 16:30.
Tuesdays: *closed*

$ €10 / €7.50

45mm, f/11, ISO 125, 1/40 sec
FF camera

4.33 Ca' Rezzonico, one of the pre-eminent galleries.

Fondazione Giorgio Cini

The Foundation has rebuilt the monastery on San Giorgio Maggiore island, housing a library of over 15,000 books on the history of Venice donated by Vittorio Cini. Located in San Giorgio Monastery, the Foundation's original plan was just to restore the convent destroyed by Napoleon, however things have expanded since then. Found inside the museum are paintings of the Tuscan and Ferrara painting schools.

Location information

⊘ Isola di San Giorgio Maggiore

⚓ S. Giorgio

🌐 www.cini.it/en

📷 @fondazionegcini

#fontaziongiorgiocini

Tickets and opening times

🕐 21st March to 20th December - 10:00 to 18:00. 21st December to 20th March - 10:00 to 16:00.

$ €13 / €10

Fondazione Querini Stampalia

Part restored palace, part modern art exhibition space, the Venetian Querini Stampalia family legacy lives on as a feature of Venetian culture. The museum recreates the opulent life of its original owners, the Querini Stampalia family. Aside from the valuable furniture, sculptures, and works of art, it also has a library with an extensive collection of books - 35,000 ancient and modern books.

Location information

◎ Campo Santa Maria Formosa, Castello

⚓ S. Zaccaria

🌐 www.querinistampalia.org/eng/home_page.php

◎ @fondazionequerinistampalia

\# #querinistampalia

Tickets and opening times

🕐 Tuesday to Sunday: 10:00 - 18:00 (last entry is 17:30).
Monday: *closed*

$ €14 / €10

Gallerie dell'Accademia

A who's who of Venetian artists have works on display here including Bellini, Carpaccio, Carriera, Titian, Tintoretto, and Veronese. In addition, Leonardo da Vinci's Vitruvian Man drawing resides here. Inside there are paintings that represent crucial moments of the civil, historical and artistic life of the city, from the 14th to the 18th century.

Location information

◎ Campo della Carita, Dorsoduro

⚓ Accademia

🌐 www.gallerieaccademia.it/en

◎ @gallerieaccademiavenezia

\# #galleriedellaccademia , #galleriedellaccademiadivenezia

Tickets and opening times

🕐 Tuesday to Sunday: 08:15 - 19:15.
Monday: 08:15 - 14:00.

$ €12 / €2

Museo Correr

Once the site of a church on Piazza San Marco, it was built as an art gallery by Teodoro Correr. During the French occupation, Napoleon subsequently turned it into a ballroom and official residences to avoid offending sensibilities if the Palazzo Ducale had been used. Converted into a museum since 1922, it displays a collection of art and the history of Venice. Visitors will have a glimpse of the Venetian daily life from past to present through the paintings, sculptures, furniture, and naval instruments.

Location information

◎ Piazza San Marco

⚓ San Marco

🌐 correr.visitmuve.it/en/home/

\# #museocorrer, #museocorrervenezia

24mm, f/11, ISO 50, 25 sec
FF camera
4.34   Museo Correr at the far end of Piazza San Marco.

Tickets and opening times

🕐 1st April to 31st October - 10:00 to 19:00 (last entry at 18:30).
1st November to 31st March - 10:30 to 17:00 (last entry is 16:30).

$ Must purchase St Mark's Square ticket (page 195) - €20 / €13

🌐 www.palazzograssi.it/en/about/sites/palazzo-grassi/

📷 @palazzo_grassi

#palazzograssi

Palazzo Grassi

Palazzo Grassi organizes important temporary exhibitions from the collection of its owner, François Pinault. This 18th century Neoclassical building was built by Giorgio Massari while some of the frescoes that adorn the staircase were created by Alessandro Longhi.

Tickets and opening times

🕐 Wednesday to Monday: 10:00 - 17:00 (last entry is 18:00).
Tuesday: *closed*

$ General entry: €18 / €15 (Palazzo Grassi and Punta della Dogana)

Logistics

⊘ Campo San Samuele, San Marco

⚓ S. Samuele

Peggy Guggenheim Collection

The home of the American heiress for thirty years, this modern art museum on the banks of the Grand Canal occupies the 18th century Palazzo Venier dei Leoni. One of the most important Italian and European art museums in Italy, it houses paintings from different genres, such as Cubism, Futurism, European Abstraction, Surrealism and American Abstract Expressionism by some of the greatest artists of the 20th century. Some famous names exhibited here include pieces by Picasso, Kandinsky, Miró, and Dalí.

Logistics

⊘ Palazzo Venier dei Leoni, Dorsoduro

⚓ Salute

🌐 www.guggenheim-venice.it/inglese/default.html

📷 @guggenheim_venice

\# #peggyguggenheim,
#peggyguggenheimcollection,
#peggyguggenheimmuseum,
#peggyguggenheimvenice

Tickets and opening times

🕐 Wednesday to Monday: 10:00 - 18:00 (last entry at 17:00).
Tuesday: *closed*

$ €15 / €13

Biblioteca Nazionale Marciana

The National Library of St Mark occupies the building opposite the Palazzo Ducale on Piazza San Marco. It contains a large number of manuscripts related to the city, as well as over one million books.

Logistics

⊘ Piazza San Marco

⚓ San Marco

🌐 marciana.venezia.sbn.it/ (in Italian)

📷 @bibliotecanazionalemarciana

\# #bibliotecanazionalemarciana

Tickets and opening times

🕐 1st April to 31st October - 10:00 to 19:00 (last entry at 18:45).
1st November to 31st March - 10:00 to 17:00 (last entry is 16:45).

$ Must purchase St Mark's Square ticket (page 195) - €20 / €13

Biennale Pavilions

A hefty chunk of Castello has been taken over for the exhibition of art, starting with Italian art in 1895. Countries from around the world have set up their own exhibitions over the years, with over half a million visitors received in recent years. It is the home of 29 pavilions designed by masters from all over the world.

Refer to the website for details of exhibitions and performances.

Logistics

⊘ Sestiere Castillo

⚓ Giardini Biennale

🌐 www.labiennale.org/en

📷 @labiennale

\# #biennale, #labiennaledivenezia,
#biennaledivenezia, #biennalevenezia,
#venicebiennale

5.00   50mm, f/8, ISO 100, 1/400 sec FF camera   *The colourful houses of Burano - look up!*

Venetian lagoon

The city of Venice, itself a set of interconnected islands, is surrounded by a lagoon of outlying spaces that have served various purposes over the life of the Venetian republic (and before). Changing fortunes, the need for space, and prevention of the contagions of fire and disease, have necessitated expansion and shifting of populations over the years. Exploring the smaller islands of the Venetian lagoon is a way to break up your time in Venice, escape the crowds, and discover some (slightly) hidden gems.

105mm, f/11, ISO 160, 1/400 sec FF camera

5.01   *Murano mimicking the Burano "look".*

 24mm, f/11, ISO 100, 1/250 sec
FF camera

5.02 The bridge leading to Campo San Donato.

Murano

Murano is the birthplace of exquisite Venetian glass art. Long ago the area was known as Amurianum or Amuriana, a group of seven islands (originally it was nine) connected by bridges. Murano was born following an edict issued by the then Doge of Venice in 1291 CE, with the aim of reducing the chances of fire destroying the city by relocating the glass foundries away from the main city.

Brick warehouses and industrial smokestacks disguise the combustible creativity held within Murano's glass studios and showrooms. Hear the eerie heavy breathing of furnaces along the fondamente (canal banks) and follow the red glow into studios to glimpse glass-blowing in progress. For shoppers, however, the main attraction of Murano is obvious: the showrooms.

▌Glassblowing in Murano

Centuries ago, the glass blowing industry of Venice was moved to Murano to prevent the city burning down, and the island fast became world famous for its artisan glass products. Today, those who still practice this skilled art tend to shy away from tourists, for health and safety reasons, as well as avoidance of distractions! Factory tours tend to see glass blowers that are predominantly "for show". 'In the past decade or so, the glass art market has been flooded by Chinese products of varying quality, however this has all-but priced out the local Venetians from the market. This is why it's often much more lucrative for factory owners to open the doors for tours rather than eke out a meagre existence on occasional sales. You'll be able to capture photos of the glass-blowing process however it may not be photos of

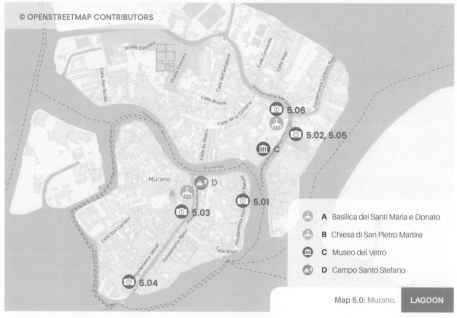

© OPENSTREETMAP CONTRIBUTORS

	A	Basilica dei Santi Maria e Donato
	B	Chiesa di San Pietro Martire
	C	Museo del Vetro
	D	Campo Santo Stefano

Map 5.0: Murano. **LAGOON**

items that will make their way to the market. If you want to purchase authentic Murano glass, and not the myriad of Chinese knock-offs sold in many of the shops in Murano (and elsewhere), look for the stamp "Vetro Artistico Murano" to indicate locally-made art.

Fortunately, this is something that Venice fiercely protects, and so this mark gives you the comfort that you're purchasing the real deal.

90mm, f11, ISO 200, 1/250 sec
FF camera

5.03 Zooming in can make scenes look "busier".

70mm, f/5.6, ISO 320, 1/100 sec
FF camera
5.04 Murano glass for sale in many shops.

Museo del Vetro (Glass Museum)

The Museo del Vetro is dedicated to the history of glass, including local Murano glass. Open since 1861 CE, the museum occupies what used to be known as Palazzo Giustinian, residence of the bishops of Torcello. The exhibitions host pieces that date as far back as the 5th century BCE.

Logistics

⊘ Fondamenta Marco Giustinian, Murano

⚓ Museo

🌐 museovetro.visitmuve.it/en/home/

#museodelvetro, #museodelvetromurano

Tickets and opening times

🕐 1st April to 31st October - 10:30 to 18:00 (last entry at 17:30). 1st November to 31st March - 13:00 to 16:30 (last entry is 16:00).

$ €10 / €7.50

Basilica dei Santi Maria e Donato

Dating from the 7th century, the Basilica of Saint Mary and Saint Donatus is the duomo for Murano island. Inside, exquisite Ravenna-quality Byzantine mosaics cover its floor and dome. Outside, the *campanile*, like most bell towers, is separate from the church. In 1125 CE, the remains of St. Donatus, as well as several rib bones of the dragon that he was alleged to have slewed, were placed in the church. According to legend, S. Donatus's dragon slaying took place in what is now Greece – make of this legend what you will!

Logistics

⊘ Fondamenta dei Vetrai, Murano

⚓ Murano Faro

🌐 www.sandonatomurano.it/ (In Italian)

#santamariaesandonato

90mm, f/11, ISO 250, 1/250 sec
FF camera
5.05 Brickwork of Basilica dei Santi Maria e Donato.

Tickets and opening times

🕐 Monday to Saturday: 09:00 - 18:00.
Sunday: 12:30 - 18:00.

$ *Free*

Chiesa di San Pietro Martire

The Roman Catholic Church of Saint Peter the Martyr was built in 1506 and still functions as a parish church. This naked brick building is popular with tourists because it houses the chapel of the Ballarin family, notable for their glassmaking skills, as well as excellent Renaissance art works by artists Bellini, Tintoretto, and Veronese.

Logistics

⊘ Fondamenta dei Vetrai, Murano

⚓ Murano Faro

🌐 en.turismovenezia.it/Venezia/Chiesa-di-San-Pietro-Martire-6128.html

\# #sanpietromartire

Tickets and opening times

🕐 Monday to Friday: 09:00 - 17:30. Saturday and Sunday: 12:00 - 17:30.

$ *Free*

Campo Santo Stefano

Campo Santo Stefano is best known for Simone Cenedese's "Comet Glass Star", an abstract blue glass starburst sculpture in the middle of the square. Next to it are the Church of St. Stephen and a 19th century Torre dell'Orologio (clock tower). Both dominate the island and can be seen from far away.

Burano

Burano is famous for its houses – it's as though the town's planners took the colour palette and cranked it up to 11! The island makes for a pleasant half-day trip from Venice, and is a key stopover during a day touring the Venetian lagoon.

Those houses!

There's no doubt about it – the colourful houses are what attract people to visit Burano these days. Legend has it that local fishermen coloured their houses to differentiate them from one another, and to recognise their own place when out at sea. The bright pastel buildings are a cute sight to behold and can even make a dreary day that much more cheerful. Owners of the houses are required to seek permission from the government to paint their house and are prescribed a set colour palette to choose from.

35mm, f/8, ISO 100, 1/400 sec
FF camera
5.07 The leaning *campanile* of San Martino Vescovo.

Venetian lace

Burano's original claim to fame was the island's intricate processing of lace. Once again, legend tells of a fisherman, engaged to a girl, managed to resist the call of the sirens. The queen of the mermaids, impressed by the loyalty of the man, presented him a wedding veil made with the foam of the sea.

24mm, f/8, ISO 100, 1/800 sec
FF camera
5.08 The flaking paint reveals "plain" bricks under.

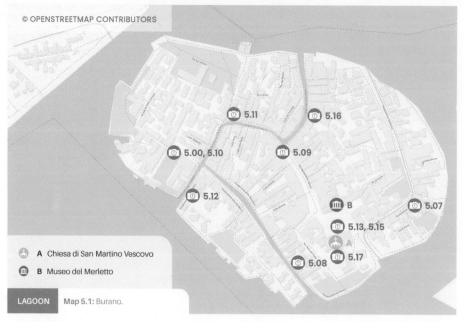

© OPENSTREETMAP CONTRIBUTORS

5.11
5.16
5.00, 5.10
5.09
5.12
B
5.07
5.13, 5.15
A
5.08 5.17

A Chiesa di San Martino Vescovo

B Museo del Merletto

LAGOON   Map 5.1: Burano.

When the bride wore the veil, her beauty was such that all the women on the island, the local women sought to imitate the design using a needle and thread. So it was that the traditional lace processing began on the island.

Sadly, similar to the fate of nearby Murano, modern manufacturing processes has rendered the tradition of hand-made lace almost obsolete. Much of the lace that is for sale in Burano (and elsewhere) was made somewhere over the other side of the world, by a machine. If you're chasing authentic lace, ask the seller for a guarantee of authenticity certificate.

Life in Burano

Tourism aside, Burano makes its living through fishing in the Venetian lagoon. You will spot locals heading out in the morning or returning with their catch towards the end of the day in their small boats. Looking up above street level reveals the day to day lives

105mm, f/8, ISO 100, 1/500 sec
FF camera

5.09   Look up as you explore the canals and alleys.

 30mm, f/8, ISO 100, 1/160 sec
FF camera

5.10 Signs of normalcy against the bright colours.

of the islanders, from life events such as birth announcements to the altane (wooden roof terraces) that afford the owner a better view over the streets, as well as a place to bask in the sun.

Logistics

Getting there - The boat ride from Venice takes around 45 minutes, and most of the day trippers arrive around 11:00. Get in early to capture the locals starting their day before the crowds arrive.

Visits in Winter - During the colder months, Burano is prone to *acqua alta* (high water flooding), so plan your trip with this in mind.

Photo tips and tricks

All-day photos - All of the brightly coloured buildings make for great photos throughout the day, including under the midday sun.

50mm, f/8, ISO 100, 1/500 sec
FF camera

5.11 *Altane* roof terraces on several Burano houses.

View from Torcello - There is a great view of all of Burano's colourful houses if you climb the *campanile* (bell tower) of Santa Maria Assunta.

90mm, f/8, iSO 100, 1/400 sec
FF camera

5.12 Time your trip to arrive before most tourists.

Chiesa di San Martino Vescovo

The main church on the island of Burano, consecrated in 1645. Its most notable feature is the *campanile* (bell tower) leaning at a rather precarious angle. The interior of the church is open to visitors, although entry these days is through a side entrance.

Logistics

⌀ Piazza Baldassarre Galuppi, Burano

⚓ Burano

🌐 en.turismovenezia.it/Venezia/Chiesa-di-San-Martino-Vescovo-6.02.html

#sanmartinovescovo

Tickets and opening times

🕐 08:00 - 12:00 and 15:00 - 19:00 daily.

$ *Free*

Museo del Merletto (Lace Museum)

The museum has over a hundred of the most precious Venetian laces on display, some of which date back to the 16th century. You can watch traditional lacemaking by local artisans, a chance to closely observe the technique of a dying art.

Logistics

🧭 Piazza Baldassarre Galuppi, Burano

⚓ Burano

🌐 museomerletto.visitmuve.it/en/home/

\# #museodelmerletto

Tickets and opening times

1st April to 31st October - 10:30 to 17:00 (last entry at 16:30).

🕐 1st November to 31st March - 10:30 to 16:30 (last entry is 16:00). Mondays: *closed*

$ €5 / €3.50

📷 105mm, f/8, ISO 100, 1/400 sec
FF camera

5.14   Burano viewed through fencing on Torcello.

📷 55mm, f/8, ISO 100, 1/500 sec
FF camera

5.15   Wells (right) were a focal point of village life.

📷 105mm, f/8, ISO 100, 1/400 sec
FF camera

5.13   Tourists in action in the heart of Burano.

 50mm, f/8, ISO 100, 1/400 sec
FF camera
5.16 Colourful houses and canals - cliché Burano!

 50mm, f/8, ISO 100, 1/400 sec
FF camera
5.17 Chiesa San Martino Vescovo, the main church in Burano.

105mm, f/8, ISO 100, 1/250 sec
FF camera

5.18   Zooming in compresses distances.

Torcello

It's hard to imagine that Torcello was once the centre of action for Venice, with numerous *palazzi* and a sizeable population. Migration towards Venice over the centuries reduced Torcello's importance, and now it's a shell of its former self. Building materials were cannibalised from here for use elsewhere hence not much to show for the island's former glory. Having said that, the island has become a place of tranquillity, and was also said to be one of Ernest Hemingway's favourite hunting sites.

Basilica di Santa Maria Assunta

First built in 639 CE, this church dedicated to the Mother of God is the oldest in Venice, shown by an inscription discovered alongside the main altar in 1895. Aside from its historical significance, the church is famous for its Byzantine mosaics from the 11th to 13th centuries. These mosaics are masterfully placed together depicting religious scenes including the Last Judgment.

Logistics

⊘   Fondamenta dei Borgognoni, Torcello

⚓   Torcello

🌐   en.turismovenezia.it/Venezia/Basilica-di-Santa-Maria-Assunta-di-Torcello-6051.html

\#   #santamariaassunta, #santamariaassuntavenezia

Tickets and opening times

🕐   1st March to 31st October - 10:30 to 18:00 (last entry at 17:30).
1st November to 28th February - 10:00 to 17:00 (last entry is 16:30).

$ €5 / €4. Including access to the campanile, €12 / €10.

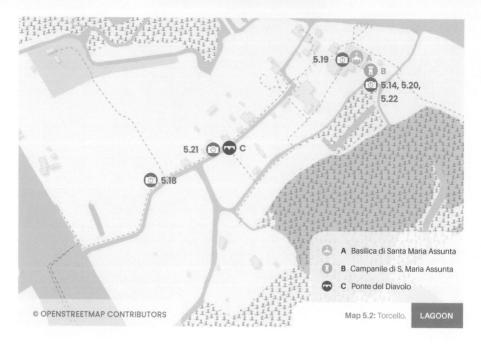

A Basilica di Santa Maria Assunta

B Campanile di S. Maria Assunta

C Ponte del Diavolo

© OPENSTREETMAP CONTRIBUTORS

Map 5.2: Torcello.

LAGOON

Photo tips and tricks

No photos inside - Unfortunately, no photos are allowed to be taken inside the basilica.

24mm, f/8, ISO 100, 1/250 sec
FF camera

5.19 Photos without tourists require a little patience.

 24mm, f/8, ISO 1000, 1/60 sec
FF camera
5.20 A wide-angle lens is best to capture the bells.

 24mm, f/8, ISO 100, 1/250 sec
FF camera
5.22 Make sure that auto-focus picks correct objects!

View from the bell tower - There is a great view of all of Burano's colourful houses if you climb the *campanile* (bell tower) of Santa Maria Assunta. However, the bell tower is enclosed by chicken wire which may require manual focusing on objects in the distance.

▌Ponte del Diavolo

A characteristic stone bridge without a parapet (rails), typical of the ancient crossings of Venice. Built in the 15th century, it has attracted many lovers of legends and mysteries every year – it was alleged that the bridge was built in one night by the devil to win a bet. The name of the bridge is instead actually a corruption of the name of a local family, "Diavoli". Much less exciting, however the legend lives on.

 50mm, f/8, ISO 100, 1/250 sec
FF camera
5.21 Ponte del Diavolo - wait for tourists to clear.

105mm, f/7.1, ISO 100, 1/400 sec
FF camera

5.23 Isola di San Michele from a *vaporetto*.

Other lagoon islands

Isola di San Michele

The resting place of many Venetians (as well as some out-of-towners), Isola di San Michele is also host to a church, Chiesa di San Michele in Isola. Dedicated to Saint Michael (in part associated with death), the church now presides over the largest cemetery that serves Venice. This is the first Renaissance-style church to have appeared in Venice.

The island (originally two islands, with the canal between them removed) was re-purposed as the cemetery for Venice after the French occupation. Napoleon consider it unsanitary to bury the dead in the *campos* (squares) of the city, and so a new centralised location was sought. Luminaries buried here include **Igor Stravinsky** (composer), **Christian Doppler** (scientist), **Joseph Brodsky** (poet), **Ezra Pound** (poet), **Luigi Nono** (composer). There are also war graves from World War I of the British Royal and Merchant Navies.

A Chiesa di San Michele in Isola

B Cimitero di San Michele

5.23

© OPENSTREETMAP CONTRIBUTORS

Map 5.3: Isola di San Michele. **LAGOON**

Logistics

Isola di San Michele

Cimitero S. Michele

en.turismovenezia.it/Venezia/Church-of-San-Michele-in-Isola-6190.html

\# #sanmicheleinisola

Chiesa opening times

🕐 08:00 - 12:00 daily.

$ *Free*

Cemetery opening times

🕐 1st April to 30th September - 07:30 to 18:00.
1st October to 31st March - 07:30 to 16:00.

$ *Free*

This is a cemetery that is in use, so please dress modestly (cover limbs) and respect the bereaved and the dead.

Photo tips and tricks

Unfortunately, photos are not permitted within the cemetery.

Isola di San Servolo

Home to Benedictine monks from the 8th century it now plays host to a small church (Chiesa dell'isola di San Servolo

and gardens. In addition, the island hosts the Torcello museum and an insane asylum museum.

Logistics

⊘ Isola di San Servolo

⚓ Accademia

🌐 sanservolo.servizimetropolitani.ve.it/en/

📷 @san_servolo

\# #sanservolo, #sanservoloisland

San Lazzaro degli Armeni

A small island converted from a leper colony to an Armenian Catholic college since the 18th century. The island has played a key historic role in Armenian studies. The still-functioning monastery, Monastero Armeno

24mm, f/11, ISO 125, 1/250 sec
FF camera
5.24   Chiesa dell'isola di San Servolo.

Mechitarista, dates back to the 14th century, and is home to a small number of monks.

70mm, f/6.3, ISO 100, 1/500 sec
FF camera

5.25   Isola di San Servolo from a *vaporetto*.

Logistics

⊘   Isola di San Lazzaro

⚓   San Lazzaro

\#   #sanlazzarodegliarmeni

Tickets and opening times

🕐   Guided tours 15:20 - 17:00 daily.

$ €6

▎Venice Lido

Today, this strip of land is the most populous of the Venetian islands. The Lido plays host to the Venice Film Festival, attracting hundreds of filmmakers from all over the world. It is also the home of protected natural areas of Alberoni and San Nicolò, where you can find rare plant and animal species including indigenous and migratory birds.

5.25

5.24

LAGOON

Map 5.4: Islands South East of the main islands of Venice.

👁 **A** Isola di San Servolo

👁 **B** San Lazzaro degli Armeni

👁 **C** Venice Lido

© OPENSTREETMAP CONTRIBUTORS

6.00   105mm, f/11, ISO 160, 1/160 sec FF camera   Gondolas moored at Gondola Traghetto di San Tomà in San Polo.

Gondolas

History of the gondola

The gondola is synonymous with Venice; the unique black boats being rowed along the tiny canals by an opera-singing *gondolier* (more on that last bit later). What has now become an expensive tourist attraction was originally a boat for domestic use by almost every Venetian family. The ancient gondolas were very different from the ones we see today plying the Grand Canal, the adaptions a result of a long technical and image evolution that has lasted more than five centuries. The first evidence of the use of gondolas was mentioned in a 1094 CE letter from the Doge Vitalie Falier to the people of Loreo. The gondola began appearing in the paintings by Carpaccio and Bellini in the 1490s. It was a status symbol of wealth, and the rich tried to outdo each other by customizing their gondolas with ornate fittings and furnishings. This practice had continued up until 1562 when the authorities banned these ostentatious displays of wealth. It was at this point that the gondola

24mm, f/5.6, ISO 1600, 1/50 sec
FF camera

6.01   The tendalin awning used up to the 1950s.

It was around this time that gondola designs started moving away from a symmetrical layout. The (now modern) design would be asymmetrical, with a custom bias based on the gondolier's weight and dimensions. This new approach was introduced by the gondola builder named Tramonlin, whose design has become the "standard" gondola in use today. A *felze* (canopy) used to be a traditional feature, shielding its occupants from the sun (and prying eyes) – a contributing factor to Venice's reputation as a city of lovers. A reduced form of canopy, known as a *tendalin* existed up to the 1950s until tourists complained that the canopy obstructed views too much!

There are now only a little over 400 gondolas left in use in Venice, almost all are dedicated to taking tourists along the majestic canals.

40mm, f/11, ISO 100, 25 sec
FF camera

6.24   Hotel Cavalleto during nighttime.

restricted to its black colour, as well as three distinct markers: the two sea horses found mid-boat, the curly tail flourish, and the *ferro* (the fin).

During the 17th century there were as many as 10,000 boats making their way around the Venetian lagoon, including many gondolas. By the end of the 19th century, the number of traditional boats in Venice reduced to around 4,000 as steam-powered boats became popular.

105mm, f/11, ISO 320, 1/250 sec
FF camera
6.03   Gondola repair at Squero di San Trovaso.

Gondola design

Construction

A modern-day gondola shares commonality with a canoe, with its flat-bottomed design ideal for Venice's canals and waterways. The construction of a gondola itself takes approximately two months to manufacture with around 500 hours of work, and costs upwards of €38,000 (plus tax). The gondola contains 280 components, and uses eight types of wood for their different properties within the boat's structure:

- Cherry
- Elm
- Fir
- Larch
- Lime
- Mahogany
- Oak
- Walnut

A modern gondola weighs 600-700kg and is 10.9m long and 1.42m wide with a 24cm bias to one side for the gondolier. This allows the gondolier to steer from one side, so will favour his size and style. The gondola typically lasts around 15 years, and another 10 after a refurbishment.

105mm, f/5.6, ISO 125, 1/500 sec
FF camera
6.04   Sea horses are a less-noticed gondola decoration.

Oarlock and oar

The distinct multi-directional *fórcola* (oarlock) allows eight different points of control of direction and speed by the gondolier. The material comes from a section of a walnut tree and carved mostly by hand by a skilled *remèr*. Like most aspects of gondola construction, the number of artisans specialising in the craft is fast dying out. There are just three master *remèri* left in Venice.

Many now purchase gondola pieces as ornaments for their homes, and a *fórcola* can cost up to €1,000.

The 4.2m *rèmo* (oar) has developed over time, moving away from single piece of wood construction to a composite used nowadays. The principle construction material is beech, with the underside made from fir. The design needs to balance the forward thrust requirement with being able to expertly navigate corners and obstacles.

50mm, f/5.6, ISO 800, 1/160 sec
FF camera

6.06 The detailed *ferro di poppa* rear ornament.

105mm, f/5.6, ISO 1600, 1/160 sec
FF camera

6.05 The unique *fórcola* (oarlock) on gondolas.

Rear ornament

The elaborate *ferro di poppa* (stern iron) ornament is known as a *risso* (curl / coil) and both emulates the movements of the oar, as well as showing off the skills of the master gondola-makers of Venice.

Gondola fin

Known by many names including *pettine, ferro di prua, fero da pròra,* or *dolphin,* the front fin acts as a counterweight to the gondolier to help stabilise the gondola, weighing up to 10kg. The design is steeped in meaning (see next page, from top to bottom):

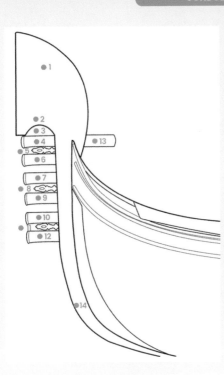

1 Cappello del Doge (Doge's hat).

2 Ponte di Rialto (Rialto bridge).

3 Bacino di San Marco (San Marco basin, the Venetian lagoon).

The six *pettini* (comb teeth) represent the *sestieri* (districts) of Venice: San Marco (**4**), San Polo (**6**), Santa Croce (**7**), Castello (**9**), Dorsoduro (**10**), and Cannaregio (**12**). The rear-facing comb tooth represents Giudecca (**13**).

The three small friezes between the comb teeth represent Murano (**5**), Burano (**8**), and Torcello (**11**).

14 Prow design references the Grand Canal.

Rowing technique

Contrary to popular belief, the gondola oar doesn't act like a punt on the bottom of the canal – the gondolier is actually rowing. A combination of technique, experience, as well as the optimised design of the gondola means that the gondolier isn't actually expending much energy when rowing under normal conditions. The use of a single oar makes navigation amongst the narrow canals much easier, as well as getting through the sometimes-heavy water traffic.

The basic technique is divided into two components, the *premier* (the "push" move) and the *stalir* (the "return" move). The gondolier's skill is in the return move, where the oar needs to act as a rudder to keep the gondola on course, without causing drag. Otherwise, the gondola would simply stay in place.

 50mm, f/5.6, ISO 800, 1/160 sec
FF camera

6.07 There is meaning to the elaborate gondola fin.

Gondolieri (Gondoliers)

During the times of the Venetian Republic, boatmen and gondoliers became part of the *fraglia dei barcaioli* (brotherhood of boatmen). Traditional gondolas required three oarsmen, with a fourth member of their team doing the on-shore administrative tasks. This has pared down over the centuries to the single-oarsman gondolas in use today.

The profession was very much kept within families, where sons would follow their fathers and brothers into the trade. Until the 20th century, gondolas were owned by Venetian families, so the gondolier would be in the employ of the gondola's owner. A gondolier came into the profession by *raccolto* (essentially being descended from gondoliers) or *trova* (the equivalent of being talent scouted).

In modern times, *gondolieri* in Venice must possess a license (there are 425 licenses available from the Gondoliers guild) and possess their own gondola. The path to getting a coveted license is not an easy one

 105mm, f/4, ISO 100, 1/250 sec
FF camera

6.10 Gondoliers greeting each other in passing.

and requires years of apprenticeship and a major exam. The results of these exams are still published in the local newspaper replete with "son of..." or "brother of..." preceding the candidate's name – an obvious nod to the enclosed male-only structure of the profession. This apprenticeship includes at least a year as what is termed a "substitute" gondolier, being on standby in case there are opportunities to cover a shift in case of illness, holiday, or bad behaviour by an existing gondolier. In a sign of progress, the first female gondolier, Giorgia Boscolo, was licensed in 2010.

A hard-working gondolier is rumoured to be able to make up to $US 150,000 per year, which is why you'll hear stories of people abandoning their university-level careers to pursue a life on the canals.

 12mm, f/11, ISO 640, 1/250 sec
CF 1.5x camera

6.11 Take multiple shots and select the sharpest one.

 130mm, f/8, ISO 200, 1/320 sec
CF 1.5x camera

6.12 View from a bridge of Squero di San Trovaso.

Squeri (Boat yards)

The Venetian Republic was a maritime empire, and ship building was always key to successfully spreading the tentacles out into the known world. Closer to home, the *squeri* (boat yards) also needed to construct and repair the various types of boats that were used within Venice itself. The biggest of these yards was the fabled Arsenale di Venezia (page 104), able during its peak to produce a completed ocean-going boat in a single day! Only a small number of ship yards are still in existence today. Owing to the decrease in need for gondolas, these remaining shipyards have opted to branch out into repair of other sea vessels to keep their doors open.

Whilst not acting as tourist attractions of themselves, you are able to visit the *squeri* and watch the construction and repair work in place during the day. You may even get lucky and be able to sneak a peek into the workshops as the *squeraroli* (master craftsmen) go about their trade.

Here are two of the remaining boat yards that you can visit.

Domenico Tramontin e Figli (Domenico Tramontin and Sons)

This family business has been in the gondola industry since 1884, and Domenico Tramontin is credited with the introduction of the changes made to gondola design that has been the standard since. The family continues to cherish the traditional gondolas' handcraft from construction to renovation; this is where many gondolas are still born. Their website has excellent English-language descriptions of the history of the business, gondola construction, and photos dating back 100 years!

35mm, f/11, ISO 160, 1/250 sec
FF camera

6.13   View from Fondamenta Ognisanti bridge.

Logistics

⊘   Calle Chiesa (end of Fondamenta Ognisanti), Dorsoduro

⚓   S. Basilio

200mm, f/8, ISO 400, 1/800 sec
CF 1.5x camera

6.14   Gondoliers' hats displayed along Squero di San Trovaso.

www.tramontingondole.it/index-english.htm

#squerotramontin

40mm, f/8, ISO 100, 1/250 sec
FF camera

6.15   Busy times in Squero di San Trovaso.

Photo tips and tricks

Good light - The workshop faces East so there is better light being cast across the yard during the morning.

Bridge - The bridge on Fondamenta Ognisanti (over Rio de l'Avogaria) gives an elevated viewpoint over the yard.

Squero di San Trovaso

Squero di San Trovaso is definitely worth checking out for those with even a vague interest in gondolas and their origins. Very much a traditional *squero* (boat yard), it has the appearance more akin to an Austrian ski chalet than a boat yard. This is because the original builders came from the Italian Dolomites in the 17th century, a time where demand was still high for gondolas and other water vessels. At its peak the boat yard employed up to 60 craftsmen, such was the demand. Now around 10 new boats are built per year, and much of what can be seen is the regular maintenance work on existing gondolas.

Logistics

⊘   Fondamenta Bonlini, Dorsoduro

⚓   Zattere

⊕   www.squerosantrovaso.com/ (In Italian)

#santrovaso, #squerosantrovaso, #squerodisantrovaso

Photo tips and tricks

Multiple visits - Boat repair work often takes place outside (particularly sanding and painting), and so check back at different times during your visit to Venice to see what activities are being undertaken. You'll need a telephoto lens to capture the close-up detail of the work being performed.

Crowds in the evening - The area around Squero San Trovaso is a popular place for locals to go for a drink along the canal after work finishes. You may struggle to get a decent vantage point of the boat yard during this time!

Sneak a peek inside - Check the back door (in Campo San Trovaso) to see if it is open. If so, you can watch the activities inside the workshop. Don't knock on the door though; you may not get a pleasant reception!

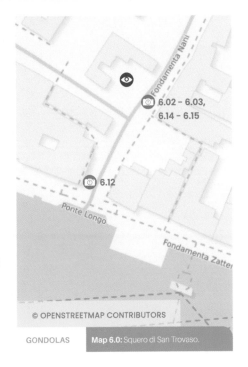

© OPENSTREETMAP CONTRIBUTORS

GONDOLAS   **Map 6.0:** Squero di San Trovaso.

50mm, f/9, ISO 100, 1/160 sec
CF 1.5x camera

6.16   Not as common, a wider-body gondola.

Gondola rides

For the majority of visitors to Venice, a ride in a gondola is one of the mustdo items on their list. The majority are then put-off by the cost, and so settle for using the vaporetti instead. There are a few dozen gondola servizio (gondola services) sprinkled around Venice, many will have gondoliers waiting to take you for a journey.

▌ The basics

All aspects of the gondola profession have been standardised, including the rates that gondoliers are expected to charge. These are set city-wide by the *Istituzione per la conservazione della gondola e la tutela del gondoliere* (Institution for the Protection and Conservation of Gondolas and Gondoliers). Whilst there are some set routes that are typically followed, there is the opportunity to discuss a custom route with the gondolier –

they may have their own "secret" route that they can recommend.

Logistics

🌐 www.gondolavenezia.it/history_tariffe.asp?Pag=43

#gondoliere, #gondolierevenezia,
   #gondoliere, #gondola, #gondolaride,
   #gondolas, #gondolier, #gondolieri

24mm, f/11, ISO 400, 30 sec
FF camera
6.19 Morning long-exposure of Gondola Bauer.

50mm, f/5.6, ISO 250, 1/250 sec
FF camera
6.20 Gondier with passengers at Bacino Orseolo.

Day tours

🕐 Tours during daytime hours (typically after 09:00).

⏱ 40 minutes

👥 6

$ €80 in total. Extra 20 minutes: €40

Evening tours

🕐 Tours during evening hours, after 19:00.

⏱ 40 minutes

👥 6

$ €100 in total. Extra 20 minutes: €50

Tips for gondola rides (or photographing them)

Busiest routes

The areas around Piazza San Marco (St Mark's Square) and Ponte di Rialto (Rialto bridge) are the most popular locations for gondola rides. It is not uncommon to see what almost looks like a conveyor belt of gondolas cruising some of the canals near Palazzo Ducale, particularly going under Ponte dei Sospiri (Bridge of Sighs).

Busiest time

Venice is famed as a city for lovers, and the period around sunset is the best time to enjoy a romantic cruise down the canals. For best visibility (assuming that's the focus of your trip!), select routes that are towards the edges of the lagoon where the sun's light hasn't been obscured by surrounding buildings. If you are set on a tour around Piazza San Marco around sunset, make sure that you book the trip in advance. This can often be done through your hotel, or by visiting the nearby gondola station during the day to reserve your tour for the evening.

 105mm, f/8, ISO 800, 1/125 sec
FF camera

6.22 Gondola setting out from Ponte di Rialto.

Common routes

We have included a set of common gondola routes so that you can position yourself in place to take photos of gondolas. Whilst you will invariably stumble across them when walking around Venice, knowing where to be and having the camera settings dialled in can help you get the best shots. Here are many of the most popular routes:

⚓ Stazio Accademia – Piazzale Roma

⚓ Traghetto Santa Maria del Giglio

⚓ Stazio Train Station – Piazzale Roma

⚓ Traghetto Santa Sofia

⚓ Traghetto Riva del Carbon

⚓ Stazio Trinita – Hotel Bauer

⚓ Traghetto Dogana

⚓ Stazio Molo

⚓ Hotel Danieli Stazio

⚓ Stazio Bacino Orseolo – San Beneto

⚓ Traghetto San Toma

 200mm, f/8, ISO 800, 1/320 sec
CF 1.5x camera

6.21 Traghetto Molo near Piazza San Marco.

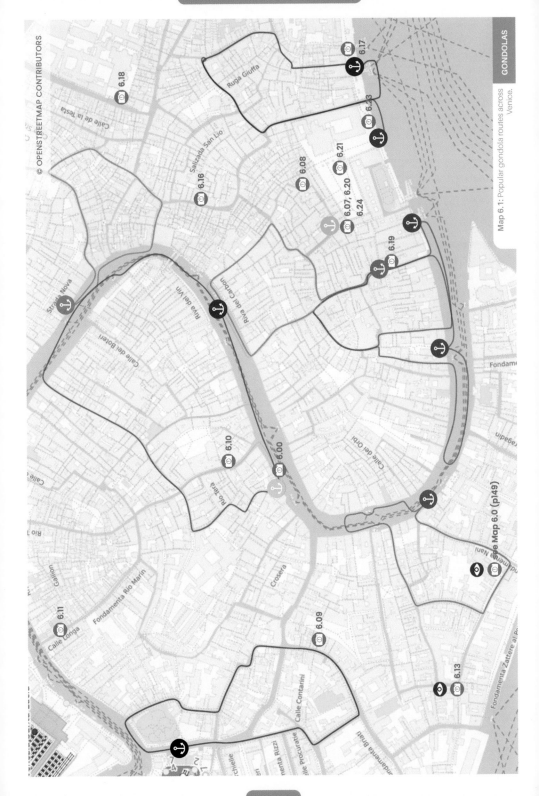

Map 6.1: Popular gondola routes across Venice.

GONDOLAS

© OPENSTREETMAP CONTRIBUTORS

See Map 6.0 (p149)

35mm, f/11, ISO 100, 25 sec
FF camera
6.23   Traghetto Molo in the evening.

Opera-singing gondoliers?

Contrary to the cliché, your average gondolier isn't going to be belting out his favourite opera classics, no matter how many times you ask! For musical and / or singing accompaniment to your gondola ride, you'll need to separately hire musicians and singers. Bearing in mind that the gondola can host a maximum of six occupants, you might need extra gondolas if you want to bring the 25-piece band!

Tip

If you're seeking a smooth ride, opt for one of the routes that make their way through the tighter canals. This takes you into parts of the city that are not accessible in any other way, and the ride will be much more physically pleasant. The gondola isn't exactly built to deal with choppy water and so isn't the greatest for comfort on the Grand Canal.

150mm, f/4, ISO 200, 1/2500 sec
CF 1.5x camera
6.02   Rebuilding a gondola in Squero di San Trovaso.

7.00   50mm, f/8, ISO 200, 1/80 sec CF 1.5x camera   Perched on a window sill, an artist is sketching life in the San Polo sestieri.

Capturing life in Venice

Sestieri (Neighbourhoods)

The main city of Venice was traditionally divided up into six *sestieri* (neighbourhoods). This division dates back to the city's early years. Each sestiere has its own character, and part of the charm of exploring Venice is sometimes trying to determine which neighbourhood you are in!

45mm, f/5.6, ISO 125, 1/800 sec FF camera

7.01   Book exchange near San Basilio in Dorsoduro.

24mm, f/11, ISO 50, 1 sec
FF camera

7.02 Piazza San Marco, the biggest *campo* in Venice.

San Marco

Named after Venice's patron saint, San Marco is the centre of Venice. For this reason, it is one of the most affluent districts; not to mention, the most visited. Although it is one of the smallest *sestieri*, most of the city's biggest landmarks can be found here.

 A Basilica di San Marco

 B Palazzo Ducale

 C Ponte dei Sospiri

 D Torre dell'Orologio

 E Campanile di San Marco

 F Piazza San Marco

 G Chiesa di San Moise

 H Chiesa di Santo Stefano

I Chiesa di Santa Maria del Giglio

J Teatro la Fenice

K Scala Contarini del Bovolo

L Museo Correr

M Palazzo Grassi

N Biblioteca Nazionale Marciana

O Campo Santa Stefano

50mm, f/2.8, ISO 160, 1/320 sec
FF camera

7.03 Setting sun over Campo di Santo Stefano.

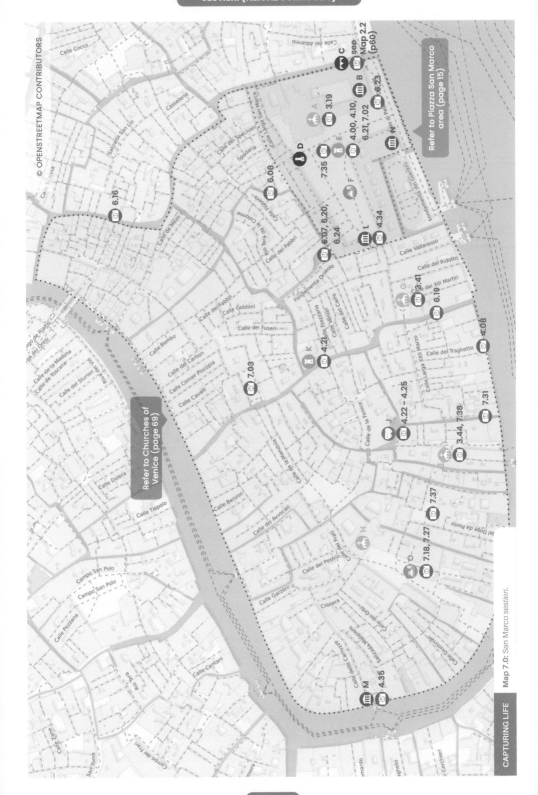

Map 7.0: San Marco *sestieri*.

CAPTURING LIFE

📷 **7.04** 105mm, f/8, ISO 320, 1/80 sec FF camera Early morning bakery near Campo San Toma.

San Polo

There is definitely an air of hustle and bustle about Venice's smallest *sestieri,* with the Rialto market and bridge being two of the biggest drawcards. The name San Polo comes from the ancient church dedicated to San Paolo Apostolo, located in the largest field of Venice after Piazza San Marco. At the edge of its borders is one of the largest churches in Venice - the Basilica of Santa Maria Gloriosa dei Frari (page 83).

📷 24mm, f/8, ISO 100, 1/60 sec
FF camera
7.06 Taking time to relax along Rio di San Polo.

📷 60mm, f/11, ISO 125, 1/250 sec
FF camera
7.05 Looking from Ponte di Rialto into San Polo.

🏛 **A** Basilica di Santa Maria Gloriosa dei Frari (I Frari)

🏛 **B** Chiesa di San Rocco

🏛 **C** Chiesa di San Giacomo di Rialto

⛩ **D** Ponte delle Tette

⛩ **E** Ponte di Rialto

🏪 **F** Campo della Pescaria (Rialto market)

🏪 **G** Campo San Polo

🏪 **H** Campo S'Aponal

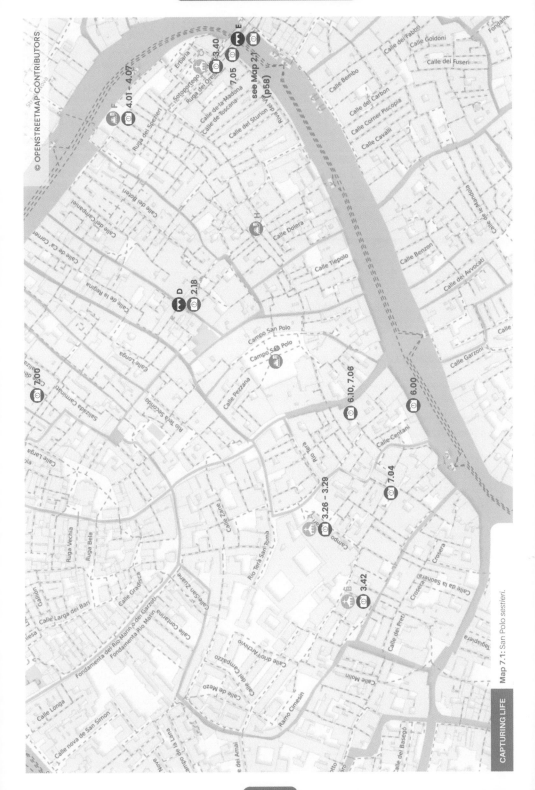

Map 7.1: San Polo sestieri.

© OPENSTREETMAP CONTRIBUTORS

35mm, f/11, ISO 320, 1/250 sec
FF camera
7.07 Quiet canal surrounding Ghetto Nuovo.

Cannaregio

Cannaregio is one of the largest and the most populated sestiere of Venice. Located in the north-west part of the city, it is crossed by long and parallel canals, and home to one of Venice's most magnificent palaces, Ca d'Oro (page 116). You can also find the Ghetto Nuovo here (page 107), is one of the oldest Jewish quarters in Europe.

105mm, f/11, ISO 800, 1/250 sec
FF camera
7.08 A small boat shed on Rio Madonna dell'Orto.

 A Chiesa della Madonna dell'Orto

 B Chiesa di Santa Maria dei Miracoli

 C Ponte dei Tre Archi

 D Ponte delle Guglie

 E Ponte della Libertà

 F Ghetto Nuovo (Jewish quarter)

 G Ca d'Oro

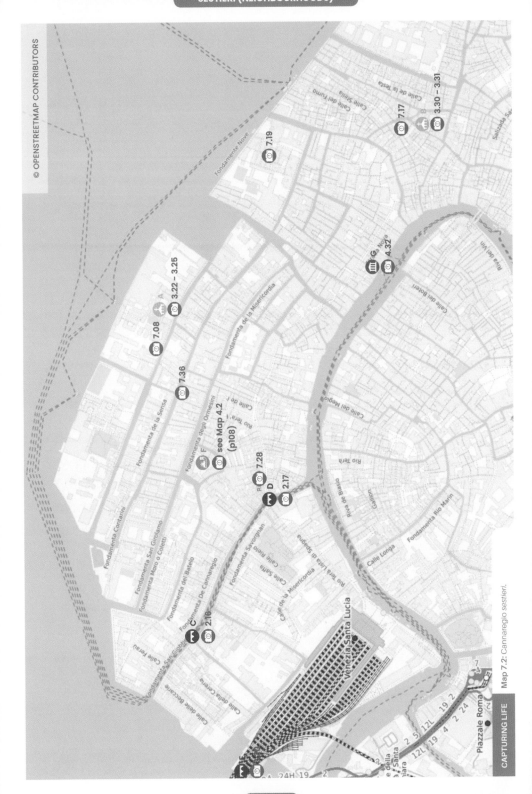

Map 7.2: Cannaregio sestieri.

CAPTURING LIFE

▌Santa Croce

 12mm, f/11, ISO 400, 1/60 sec
CF 1.5x camera
7.09 Santa Croce is good for quieter gondola rides.

Since the Ponte delle Libertà (and the preceding rail link) was built, this sestiere represents the link between Venice and the mainland. Santa Croce is the smallest and least touristy sestiere in Venice. Originally a swamp area, it has slowly grown to facilitate modern-day transport options including the ferry terminal.

 12mm, f/11, ISO 400, 1/60 sec
CF 1.5x camera
7.10 Unique building styles providing canal access.

 A Chiesa di Giacomo dell Orio

 B Chiesa di San Simeone Piccolo

 C Ponte degli Scalzi

 D Ponte delle Costituzione

 E Campo San Giacomo dell'Orio

 F Ca' Pesaro

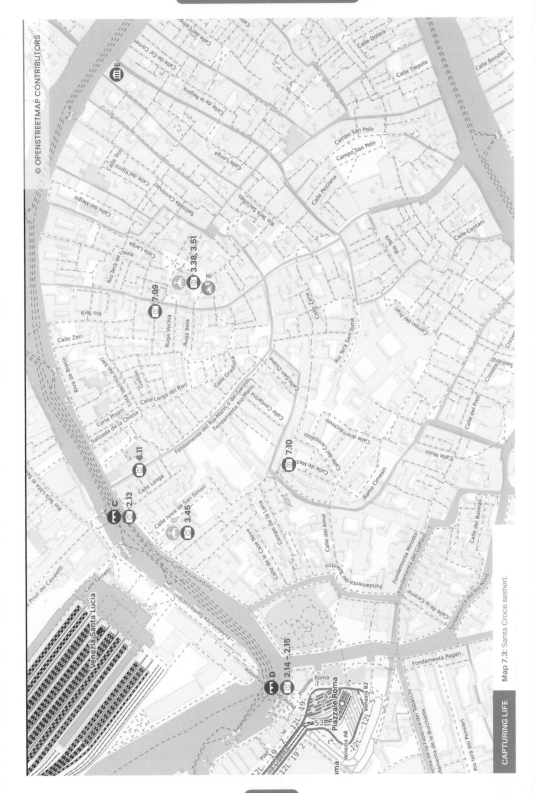

Map 7.3: Santa Croce sestieri.

24mm, f/5.6, ISO 1000, 1/40 sec
FF camera

7.11 *Sotoportego di Corte Nova* is a building passage that also served as a chapel for plague salvation.

Castello

Castello is a rather sprawling neighbourhood, with many places unexplored by tourists. It is home to the Arsenale (page 104), the largest shipyard in Venice. In fact, the naval shipyard occupies most of Castello's land area, with much of what is left being given over to the Venice Biennale (page 121).

 A Chiesa di Francesco della Vigna

 B Basilica dei Santi Giovanni e Paolo

 C Chiesa di San Zaccaria

 D Chiesa di Santa Maria Formosa

 E Basilica di San Pietro di Castello

 F Arsenale di Venezia

 G Libreria Acqua Alta

 H Museo Storico Navale

 I Fondazione Querini Stampalia

 J Biennale Pavilions

 K Campo San Francesco

 L Campo Santa Maria Formosa

90mm, f/8, ISO 250, 1/250 sec
FF camera

7.12 Signs of normalcy away from tourists.

© OPENSTREETMAP CONTRIBUTORS

Fondamenta Sant'Elena
Viale Piave

Calle del Pasubio
Calle del Carnaro
Calle Oslavia

Viale Vittorio Veneto

Viale IV Novembre
Viale Trento

Rio Terra San Giuseppe

Riva dei Partigiani

3.49 – 3.50

E

Calle Catapan
Calle Correra

7.26
7.33
7.29

Calle Stua

Calle San Domenico

Fondamenta Sant'Anna

Fondamenta Rielo

7.12

J

Riva dei Sette Martiri

4.30 – 4.31, 4.34

see Map 4.1 (p105)

7.29

H

see Map 3.2 (p80)

7.20

A

K

F

7.11

7.14
Calle Lion

C

3.37, 3.36

6.17

6.18

B

3.33 – 3.34

4.26 – 4.29

G

L

D

Ruga Giuffa

7.32

Calle de la Testa

6.16

3.47, 7.34

Salizada San Lio

Riva degli Schiavoni

Fondamente Nove

Rio del Carbon

Riva del Vin

Calle del Boteri

Salizada Nova

Fondamenta de Ca' Bala

Calle

Calle de la Croce

40mm, f/8, ISO 100, 1/125 sec
FF camera

7.13 Floating market near Campo San Barnaba.

Dorsoduro

Located at the southeast part of Venice, the Dorsoduro district (including Giudecca) is host to many of the more modern important buildings of Venice. The Gallerie dell'Accademia was constructed here, as is the Cà Foscari University, making this a bit of a student part of town. The area along the Grand Canal is also where foreigners pitched up when they decided to call Venice home, which is why the Peggy Guggenheim Collection is nestled along the canal's banks.

The large set of islands at the south end of Dorsoduro, Giudecca is a small and peaceful area often ignored by tourists. It comes to life in the summer with the celebration of the Feast of the Redeemer. Giudecca had an opulent past evident in breath taking *palazzos* with big gardens and other buildings with equally impressive architecture.

 A Basilica di Santa Maria della Salute

 B Chiesa di Santissimo Redentore

 C Chiesa di San Pantalon

 D Chiesa dell'Angelo Raffaele

 E Chiesa di San Barnaba

 F Chiesa di San Sebastiano

 G Chiesa di Santa Maria dell Rosario

 H Ponte dell'Accademia

 I Ponte dei Pugni

 J Punta della Dogana

 K Ca' Rezzonico

 L Peggy Guggenheim collection

 M Campo Santa Margherita

 N Campo San Barnaba

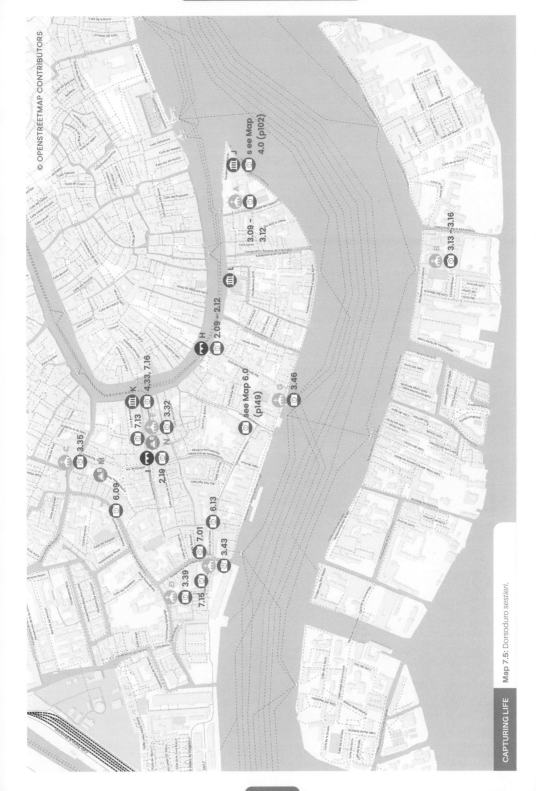

© OPENSTREETMAP CONTRIBUTORS

see Map 4.0 (p102)

3.09 – 3.12

3.13 – 3.16

2.09 – 2.12

3.46

4.33, 7.16

see Map 6.0 (p149)

7.13

3.32

3.35

2.19

6.09

6.13

7.01

3.43

3.39

7.15

CAPTURING LIFE

Map 7.5: *Dorsoduro sestieri.*

55mm, f/11, ISO 100, 1/250 sec
FF camera
7.14 The leaning *campanile* of Chiesa San Giorgio dei Greci, Venice's Greek Orthodox church.

Addresses in Venice

The postcode-type system for navigation for Venice is confusing to pretty much anybody - each sestiere has its own number that consists of four digits. Each sestiere has devised its own unique numbering, with numbers not necessarily beginning and / or ending on each street.

Thus, it is not surprising to find buildings with the same street number side-by-side, as the two buildings belong to different districts. Because of this, it can be very challenging to find a particular building in Venice.

24mm, f/11, ISO 200, 1/250 sec
FF camera
7.15 The sleepy Campo de l'Anzolo Rafael.

105mm, f/5.6, ISO 200, 1/200 sec
FF camera
7.16 A boat moored outside Ca' Rezzonico.

105mm, f/5.6, ISO 400, 1/250 sec
FF camera
7.17 A busker moving between gigs in tourist areas.

105mm, f/5.6, ISO 200, 1/200 sec
FF camera

7.18 Sunset over Campo Santo Stefano.

Campi (Town squares)

In Venice, the title of piazza has been reserved solely for Piazza San Marco (page 16). Other town squares have been relegated to the title of the lower *campo* (field). In the past, *campi* were meeting places for the inhabitants of the area as well as the place for entertainment, to settle disputes and, more recently, a playground for children. The *campo* was often where locals would draw water from a well (a central feature) or a fresh water source. It's hard to believe, however up to the French occupation, people would be buried here as well. Some of the main *campi* to explore are listed below.

San Marco

Campo Santo Stefano

Once a key market square of the city, its size alone provides a clue to this. This *campo* has numerous restaurant and shopping options. It also used to host bull fights up to 1802.

San Polo

Campo della Pescaria

The Rialto fish market is a must for those wanting to get a sense of how the locals eat at home (page 98).

Campo S'Aponal

A little harder to find (it's in front of Chiesa di Sant'Aponal), this was once the heart of the red-light district of Venice. Its alleyways and dark passage offshoots conjure up a sense of the seediness that once was. Appropriately, Ponte delle Tette (page 65) is also close by. Nowadays the square is a combination of restaurants and local shops.

Cannaregio

Campo del Ghetto Nuovo

The Jewish quarter of Venice (page 107). You can't help but recognise the sense of isolation of this area from the rest of Venice. This was a deliberate action that harks back to the days of segregation of the Jewish population onto the one island.

Santa Croce

Campo San Giacomo dell'Orio

If you're looking for evidence that Venetians live "normal" lives in the city, explore this less-

11mm, f/11, ISO 100, 1/250 sec
CF 1.5x camera
7.20 Campo de la Celestia has shaded benches!

touristed square. Watch out for kids playing football (soccer) and locals going about their daily lives.

Castello

Campo San Francesco

A quiet and shaded area with a colonnade separating the *chiesa* (page 79) from the surrounding neighbourhood.

Campo Santa Maria Formosa

An expansive space that wraps around the *chiesa* (page 94) with a few street vendors plying their wares.

Dorsoduro

Campo Santa Margherita

Another former market square, there's plenty going on during the day and night for locals and visitors alike. Fresh food vendors jostle with tourist souvenirs, surrounded by bars and restaurants.

Campo San Barnaba

Fans of *Indiana Jones and the Last Crusade* may recognise the *chiesa*, otherwise this square is usually occupied by vendors selling tourist trinkets and people on their way to somewhere else.

28mm, f/5.6, ISO 100, 1/400 sec
FF camera
7.19 An artist patiently capturing the facade of Chiesa di Santa Maria Assunta Detta I Gesuiti.

105mm, f/5.6, ISO 100, 1/200 sec
FF camera

7.21   A Venetian spritz enjoyed at the end of a day.

Eating and drinking

Visiting a city includes immersing yourself in its culinary culture and tasting the traditional dishes that the city has to offer. From succulent seafood to unique green dishes, Venetian traditional cuisine is made up of versatile ingredients that can leave you wanting more. What's difficult, however, is choosing places to go that serve authentic fare. That's because a lot of restaurants have become tourist traps, sadly something that cannot be avoided in a city like Venice.

Venetian cuisine is seasonal depending on the available ingredients. Therefore, it is difficult to find recipes based on off-season ingredients.

Types of restaurants and bars

Trattoria

A *trattoria* offers local wines in pitchers and ingredients in bulk rather than the labels of the big brands. In addition, these rustic places change their dishes almost every day to retain different foods at a good price.

4mm, f/2.2, ISO 25, 1/200 sec
iPhone 6s (CF 7x) camera

7.22   *Baccalà mantecato veneziano* (Venetian creamed cod fish) as a lunchtime appetiser.

Osterie

The *osteria* (tavern) is similar to the trattoria but specializes in serving wine or various snacks to its guests. The modern osterie, however, serves food but the menu is very limited and short. Some serve only drinks while some maintain the traditional male-only clientele.

Enoteche

An *enoteca* is a particular place where you can find many different types and qualities of wines for some aperitif or night out. An *enoteca* is not the best place to eat something or have some dinner. It's usually used by locals as a place to chat and relax after a long day at work.

Bàcaro

The *bàcaro* is the typical Venetian tavern where you can have excellent wine and other drinks. The term *bàcaro* comes from the wine merchants, the Bacari, whose name is a Venetian dialectal expression "bàcara" in honour of Bacchus.

| Local food

Baccala' Mantecata

The arrival of this fish on Venetian tables dates back to 1432 CE. The Venetian merchant Captain Piero Querini was shipwrecked on the coast of Røst in Norway and brought back the fish to the delight of locals. According to the original recipe, the mantled cod should only use olive oil, salt, pepper, garlic, bay leaves, and lemon. Today, creamed dried cod is prepared by soaking, poaching, and blending the fish

4mm, f/2.2, ISO 250 1/17 sec
iPhone 6s (CF 7x) camera
7.23   *Folpi* (Venetian style octopus).

into a smooth mousse. Then, you can spread it on bread slices.

Sarde in Saor (Marinated Sardines)

A Venetian appetizer made of fried sardine fillets marinated in vinegar with sweet onions, raisins, and pine nuts to help to balance the taste. This recipe came from Venetian fishermen and sailors who used the method to preserve the fish they caught in the days before refrigeration.

Polenta

Polenta is a legume flour or cereal cooked in water which has very ancient origins. The polenta is the staple food of Venice, adding polenta into an assortment of dishes.

Risi i Bisi (Rice and fresh peas)

The Venetians began to cultivate rice in the 15th century. Even though rice is generally associated with the Lombard and Piedmontese cuisines, it has become a staple

4mm, f/2.2, ISO 200, 1/17 sec
iPhone 6s (CF 7x) camera
7.24   *Pizza acciuga* (Anchovy pizza) - authentic pizzas are imperfect in shape and size; still tasty!

food of the Veneto region as well. The *risi i bisi* became a signature dish for Venetians as the Doges wanted it served during their feasts. A simple and easy dish which you find practically in every restaurant in Venice.

Risotto

Risotto is a rice-based dish with different variations and ingredients. Veneto risotto is cooked *all'onda* (on waves) which refers to its liquid consistency reminiscent of the water that surrounds their city.

Bigoli

The *bigoli in salsa* is a typical first course of Veneto. According to tradition, it was consumed during Christmas Eve, Good Friday and Ash Wednesday. The bigoli with sauce consists of fine slices of onions and anchovies (or sardines) slowly dissolved in olive oil. Venetian bigoli resembles large spaghetti but with a rough and porous surface.

Tiramisù

The exact origins of this dessert are hotly contested, although Venice lays some claim to its origins. The recipe has remained unchanged over the years - fresh egg, sugar, mascarpone cheese, and cocoa.

Cicchetti

This is a pre-dinner snack that goes well with a glass of wine; a Venetian take on tapas. Common combinations include olives, sandwiches, halved hardboiled eggs, or small portions of seafood and meat. By tradition, *chicceti* are eaten with fingers or toothpicks while standing.

Fritelle alla Veneziana

Similar to pancakes, the fritole (or *frittelle alla veneziana*) is the dessert of Venice. It is so popular that those who produced them

4mm, f/2.2, ISO 250 1/17 sec
iPhone 6s (CF 7x) camera
7.25
Spaghetti alla carbonara (Spaghetti with bacon, egg, cheese), a staple pasta dish across Italy.

also had a name: the *fritoleri*. Although these delicious pancakes are available year-round, the dessert is associated with the iconic Venetian carnival. During *carnivale*, you can find them in every confectionery around the city.

Local drinks

Bellini

Bellini is an Italian cocktail made of peach puree and sparkling white wine. Created in 1948 by Giuseppe Cipriani, owner of the well-known Harry's Bar in Venice, for the inauguration of the painting exhibition by the artist Giovanni Bellini. It is said that the particular pink colour of the tunic of a saint portrayed by the painter inspired Cipriani when he created this drink.

Spritz Venezia

In the mid-1800s under the rule of the Austro-Hungarian kingdom, the Austrians used to mix their wine with soda water, particularly carbonated water, since they were not used to the intense taste of wines. In their eyes, wine mixed with soda water tastes much better and Spritz (from the German *"spritzen"*, to spray) was born. This drink is now created with prosecco, bitters, and sparkling water.

Daily life

It can be hard to believe sometimes that approximately 55,000 people call Venice their home. They (sometimes begrudgingly) share their sliver of the world with the tourists, however there are ways to delve a little deeper into the day-to-day in search of more unique photographic opportunities.

▌ Markets

Venice was once one of the most important commercial centres of Europe; the city never lacked goods coming from all over the world. For this reason, there was at least one local market in almost all of the neighbourhoods. Here, people could buy not only the necessities but also a wide range of other items, such as oriental spices, precious fabrics, perfumes, and even precious metals. If you really want to know the habits and customs of a city then head to its markets where you can gain an appreciation of what locals eat and the kind of necessities that are required for life in the city. However, the never-ending rise of tourism (as well as water levels) has meant that the local population of Venice has been dwindling. Although there has been a move towards convenience

stores and supermarkets such as Co-op, local markets still exist for those in search of fresh produce and vegetables. The Rialto market (page 98) remains the largest and most popular, however here are some of the other markets to look for:

Rio Tera San Leonardo

Located in the sestiere of Cannaregio, in Strada Nova, near the Ponte delle Guglie (page 65). This small market of San Leonardo mainly sells fruit and vegetables, but there are also a couple of fish stalls. You can also find some stands that offer household items and clothing.

Campo Santa Margherita

The Dorsoduro sestiere is among the busiest places in Venice. It's not surprising because it has a market that sells fish and vegetables every morning (except Sunday and Monday).

105mm, f/11, ISO 200, 1/125 sec
FF camera

7.28   Open-air market along Rio Terà S. Leonardo.

Floating market near Campo San Barnaba

This floating market on the canal next to Ponte dei Pugni (page 65) is a great little stop for fresh vegetables and fish, and anything else that you may have forgotten to help cook lunch or dinner.

Campo Santa Maria Formosa

The Campo Santa Maria Formosa market is in one of the most popular open spaces in the city. Unlike other markets, it does not have fixed regular operating hours. There are dozens of stalls here where you can find custom jewellery, artistic glass, books, paintings and much more.

Campo Santo Stefano

Campo Santo Stefano has a bric-a-brac market where you can find many antiques and unique collectible items. At Christmas, the market is transformed into a Christmas village complete with concerts, activities, and stalls that sell Murano glass, marbled paper, olive oils, traditional food, and more.

7.29 28mm, f/8, ISO 250, 1/250 sec
FF camera
Via Garibaldi market is located near Rio Sant'Anna, including a floating vegetable market.

Via Giuseppe Garibaldi

The Via Garibaldi market is located near Rio Sant'Anna, in one of the less touristy areas of the city and serves the whole Castello district. It is a daily market that sells fruit, vegetables, fish, and also some clothes. There is also a floating market area – boats are moored daily along Rio Sant'Anna selling fruit and vegetables.

▌ Tourism in Venice

One of the realities of tourism is that there are always people waiting to sell tourists little trinkets and keepsakes of their visit, which can also be a good thing. Venice is no exception, and street vendors at busy tourist areas are a good slice of life to capture with your camera. The following tend to be the usual souvenirs on offer however please note that the vast majority of items for sale (especially the cheaper options) are NOT made anywhere near Venice.

Venetian masks

Typically worn during Carnival period each year (page 12). The masks with the long beak hark back to days of the plague, as the beaked mask was worn by doctors that would keep scents / essences in the beak in the belief that it could help ward off   the plague.

Murano glass

For greater detail, check out the Murano section (page 123).

Burano lace

Before the coloured houses became the principal attraction to Burano, the island was famous for its lace factories. Nowadays, what you see for sale is largely machine-made in a land far from Burano (page 127).

 50mm, f/5.6, ISO 125, 1/100 sec
FF camera
7.30 Typical Venetian masks (almost all made in China) are sold throughout Venice.

 28mm, f/8, ISO 1600, 1/40 sec
FF camera
7.31 Early morning garbage disposal along Rio de l'Alboro.

Additional photo opportunities

The suggested subjects below are of interest because they are adaptions to a way of life on the water. The lack of cars / trucks means that alternative mechanisms are required to move everything into, and out of, the city in a timely manner. As space is definitely at a premium, there are ways that locals take advantage of what space is available to use.

Laundry

The sight of laundry hanging outside windowsills or even across narrow streets or canals, is a common sight in Venice once you get off the tourist trail. There is some comfort in seeing this sign of the normalcy of life of Venetians. Capturing the clothes lines in the back alleys is a great way to see parts of the city that few tourists see.

Gondola replacements

Many Venetians have a boat to get about, and so the canals are full of boats of different shapes and sizes (and methods of propulsion) that are moored. Some of the manoeuvring on display to squeeze boats through tight spaces is quite impressive!

 100mm, f/7.1, ISO 640, 1/100 sec
FF camera
7.32 Venice scene paintings for sale along the busy Riva degli Schiavoni promenade.

35mm, f/11, ISO 160, 1/250 sec
FF camera

7.33 Laundry drying near Arsenale di Venezia.

Street sweepers and garbage collection

Although generally not sought out as photographic subjects, these activities take place at dawn and are completed by the time the bakeries and restaurants open for breakfast. If you're up early in the morning, the barges that are the equivalent of garbage collectors are picking up waste from restaurants and hotels along the canals.

70mm, f/8, ISO 100, 1/320 sec
CF 1.5x camera

7.35 Tourist tat for sale on Piazza San Marco.

70mm, f/8, ISO 100, 1/320 sec
CF 1.5x camera

7.34 Grotesque face at Santa Maria Formosa.

 105mm, f/5.6, ISO 100, 1/500 sec
FF camera
7.36 "Non-standard" gondolas in quiet Cannaregio.

School run

Children will be taken to school by boat and kick a soccer ball around their local *campi* after school. They generally seem unphased by tourists.

 24mm, f/11, ISO 640, 1/125 sec
FF camera
7.37 Craft goods for sale on Campo San Maurizio.

 105mm, f/8, ISO 160, 1/500 sec
FF camera
7.38 Angel on Chiesa di Santa Maria del Giglio.

Logistics

 1.52   105mm, f/5.6, ISO 640, 1/125 sec FF camera   Using a telezoom lens to compress the covered arches of Palazzo Ducale.

Planning your trip

When to visit

Venice has long been a port city for cruise ships exploring the Italian coast, or the Adriatic Sea in general. Owing to its fame, and huge list of sights, you can expect to be jostling amongst the cruise day trippers from April to November each year.

▌Expected weather conditions

Off-season - The colder months of the year are between November and March, with few tourists.

Peak of Summer - July and August are both the warmest months, as well as peak tourist season. Locals not working in the tourism industry typically go on their holiday in August.

Spring / early Summer - April and May have less crowds and less rain.

Late Summer / Autumn - higher chance of flooding (particularly in October), less crowds.

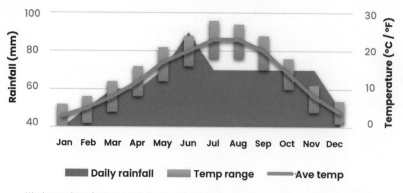

Weather conditions for Venice, including the daily temperature range, and average rainfall each month.

Light conditions

The graph below illustrates the expected light conditions throughout the year in Venice. Key points to note:

Sunshine hours - The chances of a "nice" day.

Daylight hours - The yellow bar graph indicates sunrise, sunset, and how many hours of daylight. Longer days in the Summer.

Rainfall days - Indicates the likelihood of overcast or cloudy days, as well as rain.

Festive and holiday calendar

There's never a dull moment in Venice, and the year is packed with festivals and traditions in some cases dating back several hundred years. There are plenty of photograph opportunities to be had, or just put the camera away and join in!

January

1	New Year's Day (National holiday)
6	Epiphany (National holiday).
6	*Regata delle Bafane* (The Befane races) along the Grand Canal.

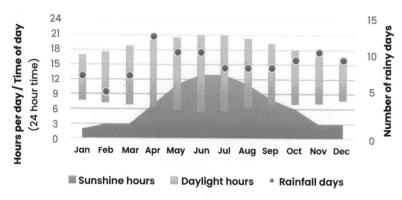

Expected light conditions by month, including daylight hours, average hours of sunshine each day.

February

varies	Carnevale - Venice's most famous masked ball festival, with events kicking off a couple of weeks before Shrove Tuesday.

March

8	*Festa della Donna* (Women's Day).
19	St Joseph's Day, also treated as Father's Day in Italy.
varies	Good Friday (National holiday).
varies	Easter Monday (National holiday).

April

25	Feast Day of Saint Mark (Patron saint of Venice), with men presenting the woman they love with a rose.
25	Liberation Day (National holiday).

May

1	Labour Day (National holiday).
varies	*Festa della Sensa*, honouring the city's ongoing "marriage" to the sea (*Sposalizio del Mar*), stretching all the way back to the 10th century. This takes place on the first Sunday after Ascension Day (40 days after Easter).
varies	*Vogalonga* (rowing race), which sees approximately 1,000 boats paddle 32km from Piazza Ducale out past Murano and Burano and finishing at Punta della Dogana. Held a weekend after *Festa della Sensa*.

June

1	Republic Day (National holiday).
varies	La Biennale di Venezia takes place every two years and encourages avant-garde artists and exhibitions from around the world.

July

varies	(third weekend) - *Festa del Redentore*, commemorating the end of the plague in 1576, in Giudecca. Walk across the temporary platform that connects Giudecca to the rest of Venice to celebrate.

August

15	Feast of the Assumption.
varies	Venice Film Festival, from the last weekend in August, held on Lido island.

September

varies	*Regata Storico* (Historical Regatta), an eight-oared gondola race.
varies	Venice International Festival of Contemporary Music.
varies	*Regata di Burano* (Burano Regatta).

October

varies	Opera season kicks off at Teatro la Fenice.
varies	Venice Marathon.

November

1	All Saints' Day.
21	*Festa della Salute*, celebrating the end of the plague in 1631. Walk across the temporary platform that connects Giudecca to the rest of Venice to Basilica di Santa Maria della Salute.

December

8	Feast of the Immaculate Conception (National holiday).
21	Christmas Day.
26	Boxing Day.
31	New Year's Eve, in Piazza San Marco.

Booking in advance

Planning your trip and making advance bookings can help make your time in Venice go that much more smoothly. Availability is definitely one reason for booking before you arrive (less important for solo travellers or going during the off season) and being able to "jump the queue" being the other. Where possible, book the following before you arrive:

Accommodation

Accommodation (page 186) is particularly important if you are looking to save money, or to attend one of the festivals (page 182) that the city is famous for.

Doge's Palace Secret Itineraries tours

The English language sessions of the Doge's Palace Secret Itineraries tours (page 45) can run out quickly owing to their popularity.

Theatre shows

If you're a fan of opera or wish to take in one of Italy's famous cultural exports, then venues like Teatro la Fenice (page 111) should be high on your list. Prices for last-minute tickets don't come cheap, and you will be losing a night of shooting the sunset, so plan early.

How to get to Venice

Venice is one of Italy's (and arguably Europe's) major tourist destinations and is well served by transport options. The vast majority of visitors staying in Venice will arrive either by air or by train. In addition, there are plenty more daytrippers arrive by the cruise ships that dock into port during the day.

Air

Venice Marco Polo Airport (IATA code: VCE) is located around 12km (7.5mi) North of Venice, and serves a large number of routes across Europe, as well as to the USA / Canada and the Middle East.

There are a few options to get from the airport to Venice itself as you exit the terminal:

Vaporetto (ferry)

Coming out of the immigration gates (after collecting luggage), look for the signs for the ferry (the boat icon). It's a 10 to 15 minutes walk to the ferry terminal along a series of horizontal travellators.

At the ferry terminal you can purchase tickets from the machine (cash / card). Lines A (Orange line / Linea Arancio) and B (Blue line / Linea Blu) depart approximately every 30 minutes, alternating between Line A and B. Note that during busy times, the boat will depart once full, with no replacement.

⏱	Approximately 60 minutes
$	€14 / €25 (one-way / return)
📅	www.alilaguna.it/en/

Tip

If you arrive and there is a substantial queue, opt for the shorter queue on the *vaporetto* leaving second. Chances are you may not get on board the first *vaporetto*, by which point, the second line is too long to join.

Bus

Coming out of the immigration gates (after collecting luggage), look for the signs for the bus stop where you can purchase tickets from the machines (cash / card). Buses heading to Venice or to Piazzale Roma terminal.

ATVO bus

⏱	20 mins
$	€8 / €15 (one-way / return)
📅	www.atvo.it/en-venice-airport.html

PLANNING YOUR TRIP **Map A.1:** Transport options for Venice.

ACTV buses 5, 35, 45

🕐 50 mins

$ €8 / €15 (one-way / return)

📅 actv.avmspa.it/en

Water taxi

Private transfers can be arranged to deposit you at your hotel or nearest port.

🕐 30 - 50 mins

$ €70

📼 www.venicelink.com/en/products/watertaxi

Taxi

A rather unorthodox choice to get from the airport to Venice! If this does work for you,

once you come out of the immigration gates (after collecting luggage) look for the signs for the taxi stands. A taxi can take you to Piazzale Roma bus terminal (on the West side of Venice), and you can walk from there.

Treviso airport

There is also the smaller Treviso Airport (IATA code: TSF), located about 31km (19mi) North of Venice, which is served by low-cost airlines. Buses are available that can take you to Piazzale Roma.

▌Train

Venice station (Stazione di Venezia Santa Lucia) sits on the West side of Venice, connected to the mainland by Ponte della Libertà. You can get high-speed train services to Rome, Milan, Naples, Turin, and Trieste, and regular services to Bologna, Verona, and other parts of Italy. Look for the "Ferrovia" signs to navigate you to the station.

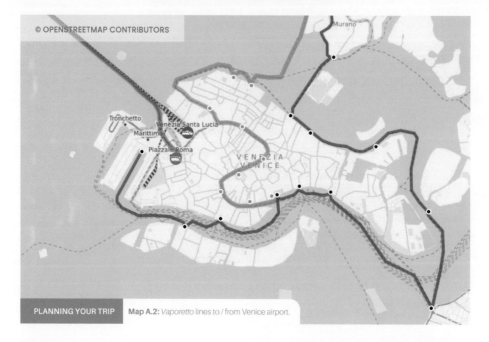

© OPENSTREETMAP CONTRIBUTORS

Tronchetto

Venezia Santa Lucia
Marittima
Piazzale Roma

VENEZIA
VENICE

Murano

PLANNING YOUR TRIP | **Map A.2:** *Vaporetto* lines to / from Venice airport.

Bus

In addition to the bus services to the airport (described above), there are bus services to mainland destinations including Mestre and Chioggia.

Boat

Ferry services connect to destinations in Greece, Croatia, and Slovenia.

Car

Part of the appeal of Venice is its car-free streets. If you have your own car, there is car parking available near Piazzale Roma. Renting a car for the period that you're staying in Venice doesn't make sense, unless you're heading away from Venice each day (still doesn't make sense!).

Accommodation

Plan and choose your accommodation for Venice wisely! There are many factors to consider, and location is everything here. It is possible to find reasonable hotels to stay in that won't be hideously expensive, however there is always compromise.

Make sure that you bear in mind the following when choosing accommodation:

Accommodation and photography opportunities

Practicalities and aesthetics can factor into your decision process for where to stay in Venice. Consider the following likely shooting scenarios, and how your choice of accommodation can play a role:

Sunrise / sunset photos

The primary benefit of being close to the places you want to see is that you can be more efficient with your time, allowing you to be in a specific place during critical times of the day for photos. Getting out of bed in time for sunrise may be a little more appealing if you don't have to travel far. And correspondingly at the end of the day, you don't have as far to go to get back to the comfort of a bed.

In summary – how far are you prepared to walk to get great sunrise photos, with virtually nobody about?

Room with a view

There is an array of hotels in Venice that have amazing vistas over the lagoon, canals, or places of action. Imagine opening your shutters in the morning to a street market that has just formed! Assuming that money isn't a limitation in your travels, consider the following hotels for great views of the Grand Canal and / or the Venetian lagoon:

- Al Ponte Antico
- Aman Hotel
- Bauer Il Palazzo
- Bauer Palladio Hotel
- Belmond Hotel Cipriani
- Ca' Sagredo Hotel
- Gritti Palace
- Hotel Danieli
- Londra Palace
- Luna Hotel Baglioni
- San Clemente Palace Kempinski

Tip

For many of the hotels mentioned above, and nearby restaurants, you can often get access to the views if you choose to dine there. Or stop by for a drink. However, you'll need to dress for the occasion, and pulling out the tripod and three cameras with lenses may not win over the staff!

Advanced tip

Consider staying in multiple hotels during your stay. This can feel a little tricky, however staying in multiple parts of Venice can be the ninja move that allows you to easily reach all of your intended destinations with minimal fuss. Moving hotels during the day isn't generally too difficult, and often it's the time of the day where light is the least flattering for a lot of subjects anyway.

Arrival time

Early morning

Arriving in the early morning means that you will have your whole day ahead of you. For most accommodation, check-in is typically mid-afternoon. However, most hotels offer the option to leave your bags at reception before check-in. If this doesn't suit you, or your accommodation is far away from where you arrive, consider using a left luggage service. These can be found at the train station and a couple of venues in the city.

Tip

If you're planning on arriving early, make sure you pack your camera equipment and a day pack somewhere that can easily be removed from your luggage. This way you can drop your luggage off and be out the door to take photos quickly. Splaying open your bags to find everything isn't the look of a sophisticated traveller!

Late at night

If possible, avoid arriving late at night into Venice. Nighttime is where things can get a little tricky. Venice is challenging to navigate at the best of times, and darkness and narrow streets aren't helpful, especially if it's your first visit to the city. *Vaporetto* and bus services start reducing in frequency towards the end of the night.

If you have no choice but to arrive late, consider booking a single night of accommodation near your point of arrival. This could mean a night spent near the train station in the city's West if arriving by train or bus. For those catching the *vaporetto* from the airport, look to stay near Madonna dell'Orto (A / orange line) or F.te Nove (B / blue line), the first ports of call when the boats reach Venice.

Departure time

Early morning

Similar to the advice above about arriving late at night, early morning departures can be tricky. This is especially the case for flights, as it typically takes around 90 minutes to get to the airport from one of the main *vaporetto* ports. If an early morning option is unavoidable, consider booking the final night's accommodation near to the airport, or consider paying for a private water taxi to the airport.

Late at night

In some respects, this can be the ideal situation! You get to spend the full day in Venice before heading off to your next destination (or home). Most hotels offer a left luggage service (most shouldn't charge for it), allowing you to utilise the rest of the day.

One point to consider – does leaving Venice late at night create complications for your arrival at your next destination?

Luggage

Venice is one of those cities where your New Year's Resolution of "carrying less gear when traveling" will pay dividends. Hauling large amounts of stuff up and down stairs and bridges, as well as threading through crowds won't get you in the best frame of mind. Leave the kitchen sink at home and rely on your minimum amount of photo gear. If you must have everything with you, consider booking accommodation that is close to a *vaporetto* port that is on one of the two lines that go to the airport, or near the train station (page 55).

Staying on the mainland

Towns including Mestre have hotel options that are cheaper than Venice, and dining options should be cheaper. Consider the following limitations:

Travel time to / from Venice

Depending on where you stay, extra time has to be allowed to reach Venice in the morning and return in the night. If you struggle to get out of bed in the morning to be in position for a sunrise photo (which is most of us), being closer to the action makes that 05:00 start much easier to pull off.

Traversing Venice

If you are arriving by train or bus (or car), your starting point will be on the very West of Venice, and you'll need the extra time to traverse the city to reach your destination.

Ambience

It is often harder to soak up the ambience of a city if you have to leave before dark to get home.

| Hotel amenities

Air conditioning

If you are visiting Venice in Summer, you are well advised to make sure that your accommodation option is fitted with air conditioning. The city gets very hot and sweaty, and the close proximity of buildings mean that the streets don't aerate so well.

Noise

The majority of hotels in Venice aren't fitted with the latest in sound insulation technologies, and noise travels down the narrow streets and alleys. For a quieter experience, look for hotels that are on side streets, not surrounded by bars / restaurants, and away from the *campi*.

WiFi

As is typical for hotels across the world, WiFi speeds in hotels in Venice are nothing to write home about. If you require reliable and fast Internet access, consider purchasing a SIM card with a generous data allowance and tether your phone to your laptop / tablet.

| Hotels vs Airbnb-type accommodation

This is definitely an option that should be explored, particularly if your stay is going to be more than a few days. The costs often are cheaper than hotels, you'll get more space and privacy, cooking space, and a peek into what local housing is like.

Logistically, finding your accommodation could prove a little more challenging, particularly if you arrive at night. If you are unsure about how to make this happen, consider a hybrid model of staying in a hotel for the first night, getting your bearings, and then obtaining the keys to the property at a leisurely hour with less stress.

Lastly, a sobering thought to bear in mind. The massive rise of the use of private accommodation options (e.g. AirBnB) has led to many residents electing to hire out their apartments and stay on the mainland. The knock-on effect has been a deterioration in the local "feel" of communities and raised prices by local vendors because of a lack of customers. This in turn affects the likelihood of other residents following suit and leaving for the mainland. In addition, the squeeze on the rental market (short-term leasing is much more lucrative) has priced out many locals, forcing them out of their beloved city.

Electricity

Venice (and all of Italy) supplies 220-230 Volts ("240V" as marked on electrical devices) and 50Hz. Wall sockets are Type L, with three-pins (the middle pin being a ground pin). European two-pin plugs that work in wall socket Types C and F also work in Italy.

Type L

Type C

Type F

35mm, f/11, ISO 400, 1/100 sec
FF camera
1.53   A bright sunrise behind the Basilica.

Check your devices before plugging them in and turning the electricity on. Most modern electronics can handle 110V-240V and 50-60Hz. For items such as hair dryers or anything with a motor or heating element in it, pay particular attention. Devices that are 110-120V won't work in 220-240V sockets.

Visas

Italy is a party to the Schengen Agreement for visas, which provide access to many European Union countries with the one visa. As requirements for visas change frequently, consult with your local Italian embassy's website (or call them) to confirm any requirement for a visa. In all cases for non-EU travellers, you will need a passport with at least six months validity left and two spaces for an entry and an exit stamp in the passport.

Government website - ec.europa.eu/home-affairs/what-we-do/policies/borders-and-visas/visa-policy/schengen_ visa_en

Italian foreign ministry - vistoperitalia. esteri.it/home/en

Citizens of 62 countries have visa-free access to the Schengen area for up to 90 days, including the majority of the Americas, as well as many Asian nations (Australia, Brunei, Hong Kong, Japan, Malaysia, New Zealand, Singapore, South Korea, Taiwan).

1.54   200mm, f/8, ISO 800, 1/160 sec CF 1.5x camera   The two "Moors" ringing the bell on top of Torre dell'Orologio clock tower.

Making the most of your time

Getting around

As you may have worked out by now, one of the relatively unique features of Venice is that it is car-free. This means that you're most likely going to be doing a bit of walking, and spending time on the water. Here are the most common forms of transport available:

Walking

The islands that make up the six *sestieri* are connected by bridges, and it is possible to spend a lot of your time in Venice simply walking around to take it all in. Navigation has traditionally been a challenge due to the labyrinthine streets and alleys, so the following are suggestions to help you out:

Map apps on your phone

Use a map app on your phone such as Google Maps, and if you don't expect to have data access on your phone, download an offline copy. The maps are very detailed and are surprisingly effective.

Signposts

Look for the signs / markers pointing to "San Marco", "Rialto", "Ferrovia" (Venice station), and "Accademia". These are the triangle (almost) of major landmarks in the city that can get you closer to your destination.

General tips

Consider navigating as though you're following a series of breadcrumbs to get to your destination. Looking on the map, select a series of waypoints such as churches, monuments, bridges, and canals to help orient you. Navigate to each waypoint in turn so avoid heading down the wrong streets.

The canals themselves, particularly the Grand Canal, can serve as landmarks when trying to determine where you are. If you're on a bridge, look up and down the canal, and count the number of other bridges or changes in direction of the canal to help pinpoint your location.

Tip

Embrace getting lost! This is probably the best way to see the hidden side of Venice, one blind alley at a time.

Vaporetto

Vaporetti (plural of *vaporetto*) are the blood lines of the city of Venice. Several *vaporetto* lines run up and down the Grand Canal, some with faster limited stop services. Arguably not the cheapest way to get about, especially for single fares, this is your sole link between Venice and many of the islands in the lagoon.

Services

Below is the summary of the *vaporetto* routes for the Venetian lagoon:

1	P. le Roma - Ferrovia - Rialto - S. Marco - Lido S.M.E
2	S. Marco / S. Zaccaria - Giudecca - Tronchetto - P. le Roma - Ferrovia - Rialto - S.Marco Giardinetti
2/	P. le Roma - Ferrovia - Rialto (and return)
3	P. le Roma - Ferrovia - Murano - Ferrovia - P. le Roma
4.1	Murano - Fondamente Nove - Ferrovia - P. le Roma - Giudecca - S. Zaccaria - Fondamente
4.2	Murano - Fondamente Nove - S. Zaccaria - Giudecca - P. le Roma - Ferrovia - Fondamente Nove - Murano
5.1	Lido S.M.E. - Ospedale - Fondamente Nove - Ferrovia - P. le Roma - S. Zaccaria - Lido S.M.E.
5.2	Lido S.M.E. - S. Zaccaria - P. le Roma - Ferrovia - Fondamente Nove - Ospedale - Lido S.M.E.
6	P. le Roma - Zattere - Giardini - S. Elena - Lido S.M.E
9	Burano - Torcello
10	Lido S.M.E. - S. Marco Giardinetti - Zattere (and return)
11	Lido S.M.E. - Alberoni Faro Rocchetta - S. Maria del Mare - Pellestrina - Chioggia
12	Venezia (F.te Nove) - Murano - Mazzorbo - Burano - Treporti - Punta Sabbioni
13	Fondamente Nove - Murano - Vignole - S. Erasmo / S. Erasmo - Treporti
14	Venezia (S. Marco-S. Zaccaria "A") - Lido S.M.E. - Punta Sabbioni
15	Venezia (S. Marco-S. Zaccaria "A") - Punta Sabbioni
16	Fusina - Venezia (Zattere)
17	Servizio Trasporto Automezzi Tronchetto - Lido S. Nicolo'
20	S. Zaccaria - S. Servolo - S. Lazzaro - S. Servolo - S. Zaccaria
22	Punta Sabbioni - Ospedale - Fondamente Nove - Tre Archi
N	S. Marco / S. Zaccaria - Canale Giudecca - Canal Grande - Lido S.M.E.

Purchasing tickets

You will need to purchase your *vaporetto* ticket from one of the main stations, either from a kiosk or self-service ticket machine. The ticket machines are located at the following stops:

- Ferrovia (Venice train station)
- P. le Roma
- Tronchetto
- F.te Nove (Fondamente Nove)
- Rialto
- Accademia
- S. Marco
- S. Zaccaria
- Arsenale
- Giardini
- Murano Colonnia
- Murano Faro
- Lido S.M.E.
- Chioggia
- Venezia-Mestre train station
- Venice Marco Polo airport

Website: www.veneziaunica.it/en/content/self-service-ticket-machines

Tickets can be purchased for single journey, as well as 1, 2, 3, and 7 days. Refer to the section on *vaporetto* passes (page 196).

Water taxi

A rather expensive option to get about Venice, a water taxi comes into its own if you are looking to reach places not accessible to *vaporetto* traffic (e.g. outlying islands). It can also be helpful if you have a large group with baggage to manage, or just want the bragging rights of paying upwards of €100 for traveling privately up the Grand Canal!

Gondola

Today, the gondola functions principally as a tourist attraction, with basic rates set by the city (around €100). Taking one of these journeys is a great way to get canal-level views of the water ways and you'll see some areas that aren't readily accessible by foot.

Practicalities

Mobile phones and internet access

SIM cards

There are four major mobile phone providers in Italy, all of which offer SIM cards on 4G / LTE band. The carriers are Vodafone, TIM, Wind Tre (a recent merger of Wind and 3), and newcomer Illiad. SIM cards are available for purchase at Venice airport, as well as in newsagents and tourist offices.

Tip

European Union regulation requires telcos to provide roaming calls and data throughout the EU using the minutes and data on your plan. This applies to prepaid SIM cards as well.

WiFi access

Hotels invariably have WiFi access, however as noted earlier (page 189) speeds aren't going to be amazing. Many restaurants and bars offer free WiFi to patrons, although you may need to ask the wait staff for the password.

Money

Putting aside the sometimes-steep prices that you can pay for food and accommodation, Venice doesn't have to break the bank. Being a little sensible about spending money and you'll be fine.

Cash

Italy was one of the early adopters of the Euro (€) at the beginning of 1999, and major tourist locations can also accept US dollars (expect to get a bad conversion rate). Keep cash for:

- Paying the tourist tax at hotels.
- Buying bottled water (if you don't want to use the water fountains) and little knick-knacks on the streets.
- Using public toilets – expect to pay around €1.50 entrance fee.
- Rewarding street performers, which is expected if you take photos of them.

Where to exchange

Most hotels offer some currency conversion services for major currencies, although rates are typically very uncompetitive. Keep an eye out for forex change booths (*bureaux de change*) near Piazza San Marco, the train station, and anywhere tourists congregate! Make sure you carry your ID (passport, identity card) as you'll need to present it when changing cash.

Banks will offer better conversion rates, although there are few Venice branches.

ATMs

Depending on your banking situation, using an ATM to withdraw Euros is usually a much easier solution than attempting to convert cash. If prompted, it's usually a better idea not to let the local bank convert the currency (and charge your bank in your home currency) as the rates aren't great.

Credit (and debit) cards

Credit cards (including Chip + PIN and contactless payment) are accepted in nearly all restaurants, hotels, and attractions. If you

wish to be cautious, you can ask to pay with card at the register so that you can keep an eye on your card throughout the transaction.

Tipping

10% (optional), if you've received good service.

Typical opening hours

Life in Venice is quite relaxed, and the city doesn't start to come alive until everyone has consumed their first *espresso* of the day and opened the doors. Most businesses don't start to open until 09:00 to 10:00. Monday or Tuesday tend to be days off for shops and restaurants. Typical opening hours are:

Banks

🕐 08:30 to 13:30 and 15:30 to 17:30 – Monday to Friday.

Museums / attractions

🕐 10:00 to 17:00 / 18:00. The most popular tourist attractions (e.g. Palazzo Ducale) often have earlier opening hours.

Churches

🕐 10:00 to 16:00 / 17:00 – Monday to Saturday. Churches are generally closed to tourists during services, although you are welcome to join.

Shops / businesses

🕐 10:00 to 13:00 and 15:30 to 19:00 – Monday to Saturday. Shops in tourist areas tend to remain open for similar hours on Sundays.

Bakeries / cafes

🕐 Bakeries and cafes providing a much-needed caffeine injection are usually open from 08:00.

Restaurants / bars

🕐 12:00 to 14:30 and 19:00 to 23:00 (later on Friday and Saturday nights). Restaurants in busy areas are open until late, and you can usually find an open kitchen up to 22:00, particularly on Friday and Saturday nights.

24mm, f/11, ISO 160, 1/200 sec
CF 1.5x camera

6.24 The busy gondola station in Bacino Orseolo is often crowded during the day.

Passes and discount cards

Venice has created a suite of discount cards for museums, churches, attractions, and transport that is incredibly comprehensive (too much for this guide!). For further details, please visit their website www.veneziaunica. it/. Reduced rates for over 65, students, and often those below 30. Below is a summary of passes that are likely to be of most interest to those in town to take photos:

General passes

St Mark's city pass

$ €28.90 / 21.90

📋 • St Mark's Square museums (see below)
• Choose three churches from the Churches of the Chorus Circuit (page 195)
• Querini Stampalla Foundation

City pass

$ €39.90 / 29.90

📋 • Civic Museums pass (page 195)
• Churches of the Chorus Circuit pass (page 195)
• Querini Stampalla Foundation
• Jewish museum

Museums

St Mark's square museums

$ €20 / 13

📋 • Doge's Palace
• Museo Correr
• Archaelogical Museum
• Monumental rooms of the Biblioteca Marciana

Civic museums pass

$ €24 / 18

📋 • St Mark's Square museums (see above), and
• Cà Rezzonico
• Palazzo Mocenigo
• Carlo Goldoni's house
• Cà Pesaro
• Glass museum (Murano)
• Lace museum (Burano)
• Natural History museum

Places of worship

Churches of the Chorus circuit

$ €12 / 8

📋 • Santa Maria del Giglio
• San Stae
• Santo Stefano
• Sant'Alvise
• Santa Maria Formosa
• San Pietro di Castello
• Santa Maria dei Miracoli
• Santissimo Redentore

- S. Giovanni Elemosinario
- Santa Maria del Rosario (Gesuati)
- San Polo
- San Sebastiano
- Santa Maria Gloriosa dei Frari
- San Giacomo dall'Orio
- San Giobbe
- San Giuseppe

Jewish museum + guided tour of synagogues

$ €12 / 10

Includes access to the Jewish museum, and a guided tour of three of the five Synagogues in the New and Old Ghettos. Note: The Synagogues cannot be visited without a guide.

| Public transport

Vaporetto + bus (Lido)

Covers ACTV transportation within Venice and the lagoon islands. Excludes trips to / from Venice airport.

$
- 1 day (24 hours) - €20
- 2 days (48 hours) - €30
- 3 days (72 hours) - €40
- 7 days - €60

Single ride fares are €7.50, and so three rides in a day justifies a one-day pass.

Tip

If you only have one return boat trip in mind (i.e. visiting one island), consider purchasing a one-day pass. By purchasing the unlimited travel option, it makes you consider possibilities of island-hopping to take in additional locations.

Language

The Venetian language is considered a separate Romance language to modern day Italian. Venetian is spoken by approximately four million people across the region (and the world). Italian will be universally understood by locals, and you won't have any issues with English either.

Tip

As a rule of thumb, the more languages you see on the restaurant / bar menu, the more tourist-oriented the establishment will be. Don't let this put you off, as the food and service can still be top-notch. Even if you move away from the crowds of Venice, you'll be unlikely to find places that don't have English menus available.

Staying healthy

| Drinking water

The water that comes from the taps in Venice is safe to drink, as is the water that spouts from the fountains in the *campi*. Ideally you should carry a water bottle and refill it whenever you get a chance, as purchasing water is going to be expensive over time.

Whatever you do, resist any temptation to drink or make contact with the water in the canals and Venetian lagoon. A lot of effluent and engine oils etc run into the water, and skin contact can lead to irritation or infection.

Flooding

Floods are an unfortunate reality of life living on the Venetian lagoon, with buildings built on a largely sedimentary foundation. If you come across *passarelle* (pedestrian platforms) being laid out as you are exploring the area, this is a strong indicator that an *acqua alta* (high water) is looming. It is not unheard of for children to swim in the water, or others to be up to their knees (or worse) wading through. It is also likely to affect opening times for key attractions in the neighbourhood.

No barriers

Many of the canals around Venice do not have walls or barriers and ending up in the drink is relatively common (alcohol is generally involved!). The risk is mentioned here because as photographers it is easy to get distracted by your surroundings. One step in the wrong direction during the excitement, and you'll be clamouring to see if your travel insurance covers water damage.

In addition, take care when pavements are slippery, or when there are many people bustling past.

Sun

Wearing a hat, sun cream, and sunglasses makes sense, particularly if you are going to be on the water. The reflected light from the water has a nasty habit of catching people by surprise when they assume that a hat is sufficient to protect their skin.

Sore feet / ankles

Your feet are going to be your main form of transport in Venice, and they will indeed get used! Comfortable shoes and socks make sense and carry some plasters in case you feel a sore developing. This is especially important in the warmer months as your feet will get very hot over the course of the day. Most *campi* have benches to sit, some of them are even shaded. During the warmer months, churches are cool and calm places to relax and catch your breath while you take in the surroundings.

Toilets

There are a few public toilets around the city, mostly next to main tourist attractions. Entry is €1.50 (coins only), and the facilities are kept clean.

Tip

Assuming you don't have one of the many museum or venue passes (page 195), consider popping into one of the museums or galleries to use the bathroom facilities. Entry to most places is typically a few Euros, and you've now got access to one more place to indulge in the history and culture of the city.

A brief history of Venice

The area off the Italian coast that was to become Venice is a lagoon of mudflats, formed by the estuaries of three rivers in Northern Italy. Sand and mud are washed up by the Adriatic Sea creating long and thin islands which protect the lagoon. This was to become the home of the Venetian Republic which, for many centuries, was one of the most powerful influences in Europe.

What is now Venice started to take form around 400 CE when Italian refugees fled Attila the Hun's reign of terror. They began to build houses made of wattle and daub, with posts driven into the mud and anchored with woven tree branches. Most of these refugees became fishermen and engaged in trading and drying seawater to make salt. While Venice did not have natural resources apart from salt, the location became the advantage – Venice was protected by their strategic position which made attacks of the lagoon difficult.

The Venetians learned how to move merchandise and handle ships; they had become trading experts. Evidence of this is none other than Marco Polo, who played a significant role in the opening of trade routes, particularly to China. By the 9th century, Venice was already a city state and was one of the key maritime republics in Europe.

The Venice Arsenal (*Porta Magna*) was established in 1104 CE. It was a state-owned complex of armouries and shipyards, located in the district of Castello. It was proof of Venice's naval power and was considered one of history's earliest industrial enterprises due to its sheer scale. The city benefitted from the use of its ships and soldiers during the Crusades.

As Venice continued to flourish in trade and maritime prowess, a fourth crusade to the Holy Land was proposed in 1199. The Venetians agreed to build ships for the Crusaders, which the army was unable to pay. To settle the debt, the Venetians persuaded the Crusaders to help them attack Constantinople in 1204. The resulting attacks helped to expand Venetian territory.

However, a combination of factors started to lead to the decline of Venice and its influence over the centuries. A series of plagues between the 14th and 17th centuries wiped out swathes of the population at a time. Venice's fabled navy and merchant ships failed to keep pace with changes in technology, leaving Venice unable to conquer the oceans. European seafaring nations were all able to bypass the trade routes that had created wealth for Venice for so long.

Venice was, however, able to keep itself relevant within Europe through its intellectual and artistic pursuits. Venice became the printing capital of Europe in the 15th century, and in the centuries after, Venice cemented its reputation for being the home of master artists, as well as promoting its style of architecture.

In 1797, Napoleon came knocking, and conquered Venice as part of his campaign against the Austro-Hungarian Hapsburgs. That year marked the end of the Venetian Republic, and a provisional democratic municipality was established in its place. This lasted until the fall of Napoleon, and in 1815, Venice became part of the Austrian empire – this was not a good time for the city.

Venice (along with the rest of the Veneto region) was to change hands one last time; it became part of the newly formed Italy in 1866. Venice flourished once again as a port and as a manufacturing centre by the end of the 19th century. Venice was spared the worst of the ravages of World War II. Sadly however, its Jewish population were deported, and very few survived the Nazi concentration camps.

Post-World War II, Venice continued its battles with the sea, and in November 1966 experienced what was considered the worst floods in the city's history. Piazza San Marco was 1.5m underwater! The efforts of UNESCO and other organisations helped to reverse the 150 years of neglect that the city had suffered after the fall of the Venetian Republic. Further efforts have taken place over the years to introduce flood gates and other measures to reduce the effects of high tides in the city. Sadly, these measures have come at massive cost, with corruption often being blamed for budget and timeline blowouts.

The other big problem facing Venice is the effects of over-tourism. As described elsewhere in this guide, the average Venetian is being financially squeezed out of their homes and community. Measures are being taken to reduce the impact of cruise ships and to encourage tourists to spend money in the city beyond the vicinity of Piazza San Marco.

Index of maps

Index of locations

Walkabout photo guides

About us

Walkabout photo guides was founded with the express mission of enabling budding travel photographers to get out and explore new places and come home with great photos!

We combine experience on the ground with extensive research, distilling it into a coherent structure, saving the reader hours of time. Our guides enable the reader to confidently be on top of the logistics of a trip focused on taking photos (which is often different to a holiday).

No matter whether you're a weekend warrior, digital nomad, or first-time traveller, our guides will shortcut a lot of the planning and logistics that can stand in the way of getting great travel photos.

About the author

James Dugan was born and raised in Australia. Being based in London for many years, Venice was high on his destination list. It was love at first sight on the first trip. James has subsequently travelled to Venice over the years to experience the different seasons and embrace the possibility of getting lost along the way!

walkaboutphotoguides.com